Bill Peach's
GOLD

Bill Peach's
GOLD

M

Designed by Tony Denny
Edited by Helen Findlay and Nina Riemer
Photographs by Bill Peach and Shirley Peach

Cover painting: 'The Prospector', Julian Ashton, Gulgong Museum.
Reproduced by permission of the Julian Ashton Art School.
'The Last of England', Ford Maddox Brown. By courtesy
of Birmingham Museum and Art Gallery, England.

The ABC gratefully acknowledges illustration sources
including the Mitchell Library, the Dixson Library,
La Trobe Library, Holtermann Collection, the
Melbourne University Gallery, the National Library of
Australia and the Gulgong Museum.

This first edition published 1983

Published jointly by the Australian Broadcasting Commission
and The Macmillan Company of Australia Pty Ltd

The Australian Broadcasting Commission
145-153 Elizabeth Street, Sydney 2000

The Macmillan Company of Australia Pty Ltd
107 Moray Street, South Melbourne 3025
Associated companies in London and Basingstoke, England
Auckland, Dallas, Delhi, Hong Kong, Johannesburg, Lagos,
Manzini, Nairobi, New York, Singapore, Tokyo, Washington,
Zaria

National Library of Australia
cataloguing in publication data:
Peach, Bill, 1935–
    Gold

    ISBN 0 333 33921 5 (Macmillan Australia)
    ISBN 0 642 97399 7 (Australian Broadcasting Commission)

    1. Gold. 1. Australian Broadcasting Commission
    2. Title.

    553.4'1

Printed in Australia by Griffin Press Limited, Adelaide
Typeset by Dalley Photocomposition
Text: Aster 11 on 13

Contents

Author's Note

Australia switched to decimal currency in 1966. The new unit of currency, the Australian dollar, was made the equivalent of ten shillings, or half of one pound, in the old currency. I don't question the wisdom of the change, but it presents a real bugbear to anyone writing about money values of a century and more ago. It would be quite misleading to say that £1 in 1851 equals $2 in 1983. Both the price of gold and the average Australian wage are now fifty times more than they were in the days of the gold rush. The purchasing value of £1 in 1851 was equivalent to about $100 in today's money. The four ounces of gold found by Lister and Tom at Ophir would be worth around $1600 today, and the reward given to Hargraves, just over £12,000, represents over a million dollars in modern currency.

So while I have quoted modern gold production values in modern currency, I have left the references to the previous century in the language and the currency of that time, while occasionally drawing a comparison with today's money values. I have quoted gold production in ounces throughout, because the ounce is still the accepted unit for gold pricing on the world market.

Bill Peach

Introduction

William Charles Wentworth

Gold was crucial in Australia's history. It was not our first source of wealth, nor our first mineral to be mined, but it was the catalyst that created the idea of Australia as a country where every man could seek his own fortune.

Gold changed the image of Australia overseas. It tripled the population of Australia and it changed the physical face of Australia, creating inland civilisations on what had been vast sheep runs and generating enormous wealth which was soon reflected in the opulence of capital and provincial cities.

Gold brought new kinds of people to Australia, ended convict transportation to the eastern States, created new transport networks and hastened the introduction of representative democracy.

These developments were not greeted with universal joy. When the gold discoveries of 1851 were announced, John Fairfax told his *Sydney Morning Herald* readers that they threatened 'calamities far more terrible than earthquake or pestilence'.

The calamity the colonial conservatives feared was democracy itself. William Wentworth in 1851 said he 'regretted to find there was a spirit of democracy about, which was daily extending its limits'. When his proposals to create a colonial aristocracy were howled down, Wentworth grumped off to live in England, muttering about 'levelling principles, selfishness, ignorance and democracy'. Apparently his desire to enshrine himself and his fellow squatters as the permanent rulers of the land was not selfishness, but opposition to that desire was.

The extraordinary reactions of men like Fairfax and Wentworth to the gold discovery indicate that Australia's

7

progress on all fronts would have been much less impressive if gold had *not* been found here. The discovery was probably the luckiest event in the history of a remarkably lucky country.

I wish to thank all the people, too numerous to name individually, who have helped me in this project. Many of our ancestors were pioneers in the search for gold. I believe their story is worth telling and I hope that it adds something to our understanding of Australia.

Finders Keepers

The Tip of the Top, as locals call the tip of Cape York, is the northernmost point of the Australian continent. Just to the west of it is a small, wedge-shaped, hilly island called Possession Island. Few Australians have heard of it and there are even fewer who have seen it, but one of the most important ceremonies in Australian history took place on that lonely island.

It was there that Captain Cook, after his epic voyage of exploration along a vast and uncharted coastline, formally claimed possession of eastern Australia for the British Crown. He described the events of August 22, 1770, in his journal:

> We were in great hopes that we had at last found a passage into the Indian seas, but in order to be better informed I landed with a party of men accompanied by Mr. Banks and Dr. Solander upon the island which lies at the southeast point of the passage. I went upon the highest hill and satisfied myself of the great probability of a passage through which I intend going with the ship, and therefore may land no more upon this eastern coast of New Holland. I now once more hoisted English colours and in the name of His Majesty King George the Third took possession of the whole eastern coast by the name of New South Wales after which we fired three volleys of small arms which were answered by the like number from the ship.

It was a momentous day in Australian history. But it would have been more momentous if Cook had found what was right under his flagstaff. Had they known, his sailors, instead of firing shots, would have been up on the hill like a shot.

Possession Island

In 1895, a century and a quarter after Captain Cook's ceremony, gold was discovered on Possession Island. The first shaft was sunk on top of the highest hill, on the exact spot where Cook had planted his flag, and 2480 ounces of gold were mined from the island.

If Cook had dug a little deeper European settlement of Australia might have begun with a gold rush to Cape York, not with a convict fleet to Botany Bay. Australia might have become a New World to eclipse the American colonies. Instead it became a prison. But the destiny of the country was eventually to change dramatically. And when it happened, the cause of the change was gold.

*A precious gold ornament,
a Jewish Menorah,
Sovereign Hill Museum,
Ballarat*

Gold, the mysterious element from the molten centre of the planet, solidified over long ages into reefs in the earth's crust, has fascinated mankind since the beginning of recorded history. It has always been the most enduring and alluring of metals, the stuff of myth and legend, the index of value, and the visible manifestation of wealth.

Ancient civilisations—the Sumerians and Egyptians, the Persians and the Hebrews—prized gold and learned how to mine it and how to work it into beautiful shapes. Their nobles sported it as ornament. Their temples and their royal tombs were filled with it. King Croesus of Lydia had it made into coins to form the world's first fixed currency.

Gold was wealth and fortune, though not everyone's good fortune. Wars were fought for it, empires conquered for it, people enslaved for it, the Americas invaded for it.

There was one continent which remained unknown to Europeans, though they reasoned it must be there. They called it Terra Australis Incognita, the unknown south land. But Asian legend spoke of a land of gold there— Locach, or Beach, or Maletur—and these names began to appear on maps. Marco Polo wrote:

> There standeth the country named Locach, great and rich. They speak the Persian tongue and worship idols. They pay no kind of tribute to any man for there is no man that can do them hurt. There is found great plenty of gold and a great number of the small white shells of the sea, which is used in some places instead of money. Also, there be many elephantes. Unto this island there cometh very few strangers, for that it standeth out of the way.

Perhaps the Portuguese came this way. Their Dauphin chart of the 1530s showed north-west Australia as the Costa d'Ouro—the Gold Coast. But the Dutch, it seemed, had laid these legends to rest when they charted the coast of New Holland. Instead of great plenty of gold, they found great plenty of flies, and nomadic natives with nothing of value to trade.

Cook recorded that these people lived by values of their own:

> From what I have seen of the natives of New Holland, they may appear to some to be the most wretched people upon earth but in reality they are far happier than we Europeans. They live in a tranquillity which is not disturbed by the inequality of condition. The earth and sea of their own accord furnishes them with all things necessary for life, they covet not magnificent houses.

Nor did the Aboriginals covet gold. But their tranquillity was soon to be wrecked by people who did.

The convicts were keenly interested in gold. Some of them had tried to mine it from other people's pockets. Their reward was a trip to Botany Bay. There, they remained under suspicion. In August 1788, a convict named Daley produced a lump of gold-bearing earth which he said he'd found in the bush by the Harbour. Daley was made to

The Chain Gang

admit that he'd filed down a brass buckle and a golden guinea to manufacture his specimen. The first man to claim to have found gold in Australia was rewarded with 300 lashes for his impudence.

Botany Bay was hardly a golden beginning. The metal that most concerned the convicts was the iron of the chain gang. The challenge was to survive. When the prison walls were pushed back by the first road over the Blue Mountains to Bathurst, the convict road gangs found bits of gold turned up by their picks. They learned to keep quiet about it. It was better than being accused of stealing it and getting flogged.

The first official and respectable report of gold came from west of the Blue Mountains, on the Fish River at Locksley, near Bathurst. Assistant-surveyor James McBrien recorded in his field book:

> February 15, 1823. At east 1 chain 50 links to river and marked gum-tree. At this place I found numerous particles of Gold in the sand in the hills convenient to the river.

The Colonial Government in Sydney did nothing about this report, and McBrien said no more. The next two claimants were not so silent.

The Polish explorer and self-styled Count, Paul Strzelecki, claimed he'd found gold in the Blue Mountains near Hartley in 1839, and reported it to Governor Gipps. But, he complained, the Governor had squashed him:

> I was frightened by Sir George Gipps, and was gagged without being bribed, but my papers and the memorandum of Sir George Gipps must be in the records of the colonial despatches—who knew all about it, but remained silent! I was cheated out of the reward!

A parson and amateur geologist, the Reverend William

13

Branwhite Clarke, said that he had found Blue Mountains gold at Hassan's Walls and had shown it to Governor Gipps in 1844, but with mortifying results. Gipps, he claimed, had dismissed him with the terse sentence: 'Put it away, Mr Clarke, or we shall all have our throats cut!'

Was Governor Gipps terrified that gold would cause a convict uprising in New South Wales? Was he blind to the benefits gold might bring to Australia? Both Strzelecki and Clarke gave their accounts of their exchanges with Gipps some years later, when they were trying to rescue their own reputations and claim a share of credit for the discovery of gold. Gipps was no longer alive to give his side of the story. Perhaps he didn't say those things. Perhaps he was just cautious, preoccupied with matters that he and most other people thought more important at that time.

Australia had long ceased to be a mere convict colony. The business of the country was wool. For thirty years, the squatters and pioneers with their herds and primitive bullock drays had pushed into the country further out. The job as they saw it was to conquer the bush and bring home the Golden Fleece. It was a way of life as ancient as the Bible. The shepherds guarded the flocks, and the squatters, those old patriarchs of Australia, guarded the shepherds and tried to keep their minds on the job.

Some shepherds, like old McGregor from Wellington on the Macquarie, sold bits of gold to Sydney jewellers, but wouldn't tell where they had got the gold. On a creek near Beechworth, Victoria, in 1846, men digging a millrace found some yellow specks and said, 'Look! It's gold!'

The squatter, David Reid, said, 'No, it's mica. Throw it away and get on with the job'.

It *was* gold, and it was just one of a dozen finds that might have started an Australian gold rush before 1850. But Australia was not thinking gold. It was a find in a millrace exactly like the one at Beechworth which changed the course of Australian history, but it happened on the other side of the Pacific Ocean.

GOLD MINE FOUND

In the newly made raceway of the sawmill recently erected by Captain Sutter on the American Fork, gold has been found in considerable quantities. California no doubt is rich in mineral wealth. Great chances here for scientific capitalists.

Reverend William Branwhite Clarke

Opposite top: *The American River at Coloma*
Opposite bottom: *Captain Sutter and James Marshall*

Captain John Sutter

14

That brief paragraph on March 15, 1848, in an obscure San Francisco paper called *The Californian*, heralded the first great gold rush of modern times. It happened at Coloma, on the American River, in the foothills of the Sierra Nevadas, and the way it happened had many strange parallels with Australian history.

California in the 1840s was a remote and thinly settled territory of Mexico. Sutter's Fort, on the Sacramento River, was the headquarters of Captain John Sutter, a Swiss-German who had obtained a big grant of land from the Mexican governor and was on his way to becoming a prosperous sheep and cattle rancher. Further inland, on the American River, Sutter had his men build a sawmill. It was to supply the timber to build his planned settlement at Sacramento. The men dug a race or channel to drive the waterwheel, and they ran river water through to deepen it and push out the gravel.

One morning in January 1848, Sutter's foreman James Marshall looked in the millrace and said, 'Boys, by God, I believe I've found a goldmine!' Today, at Coloma, his statue is there, pointing to the spot where he made a discovery that changed the world. The expression on his face is not very happy and that's understandable. It did not turn out to be a lucky strike for him, nor for Captain Sutter.

Like the workmen at Beechworth in Victoria, Marshall found gold in a millrace, and like them, he showed it to his boss. But unlike the grazier Reid, the grazier Sutter tested it and proved it *was* gold. Sutter didn't know what to do. He could foresee trouble for his pastoral kingdom, and he tried to hush up the discovery. In fact, the news didn't get published for a couple of months after a drunken teamster from Coloma had paid for some store goods with gold. Even then the rush didn't start till the shrewd storekeeper, Sam Brannan, cornered all the hardware in picks and shovels, and rode through the streets of San Francisco brandishing a jar of Coloma gold and shouting, 'Gold! Gold! Gold from the American River!'

The moral was later to apply in Australia. It wasn't finding gold that counted; it was how much noise you made about it. When the rush did start, Sutter and Marshall were pushed out and ruined, Brannan became a millionaire, and America went ahead like a rocket. By an incredible stroke of fortune, the United States had formally wrested the territory of California from Mexico just before the

Gold diggers approaching San Francisco

news of the gold discovery was announced.

> *I'll scrape the mountains clean, old gal,*
> *I'll drain the rivers dry,*
> *I'm off to California,*
> *Susannah, don't you cry.*
>
> *Oh, Susannah, don't you cry for me,*
> *I'm off to California with*
> *A washbowl on my knee.*

Gold towns like Rough and Ready, Angel's Camp, Hangtown, Coyote Diggings, Mad Mule Gulch and Rattlesnake Bar sprang up all through the Mother Lode country on the slopes of the Sierra Nevada. Columbia became California's second largest city with forty saloons and 159 gambling dens, and countless fandango halls where the miners cavorted with Mexican dancing girls. There was plenty of gold about. Ten million dollars' worth was mined in 1849, and a few miners dug out thirty thousand dollars' worth in a week.

Even fewer managed to keep their fortunes. Goldfield prices were astronomical—a pair of boots was thirty dol-

17

lars, potatoes and onions a dollar each. And what the storekeepers didn't get, the saloons usually did. For every man who struck it rich, there were hundreds who just made wages, for all the hard work of mining and the hard winters of California.

But the gold rush did wonders for America. It poured millions of dollars into a depressed economy and greatly sped up the expansion of the nation. California became a state of the union with the motto 'Eureka' (I have found it), and the United States for the first time stretched from sea to shining sea. The world and in particular Australia looked at California in wonder. This was what gold could do for a country.

The first effect of the gold strike was to empty the little village of San Francisco. Every able-bodied man rushed away to the American River. But as the news spread round the world, San Francisco became the port for the biggest mass movement of people and the wildest mass mania since the crusades. Population rose from fifteen hundred to fifteen thousand in one year.

Top left: *San Francisco Harbour*
Bottom left: *The Californian Seal 'Eureka'*
Top right: *Miner Forty-Niner cabin, Columbia*
Bottom right: *Gold ingots in the old San Francisco mint*

The miners 'forty-niners came from everywhere—across the Pacific from Australia and China, overland and through the Panama jungle from the American east, around Cape Horn from Europe. By the end of 1849, 300 ships had arrived in San Francisco harbour. The crews abandoned ship as a matter of course, without even waiting to unload the cargo before they raced off to the goldfields. The ships were left rotting at anchor in the Bay.

The first Sydney ship sailed for California in January 1849, carrying mostly stores, but as the get-rich-quick stories came back, passengers rushed the ships, and in 1850 the port of Sydney sent more than 200 ships to San Francisco. Eastern Americans had to sail eight months round Cape Horn or struggle 2000 miles overland to reach California, but it was an easy seventy-day trip from Sydney. Seven thousand people took it—most of them adventurous able-bodied men Australia could ill afford to lose.

Old San Francisco, corner of Sacramento and Powell Streets

There were a few that she could well afford to lose—ex-convicts called the Sydney Ducks. They lived in a seedy quarter on Telegraph Hill called Sydney Town. They were accused of dreadful crimes, including setting San Francisco on fire. Four of them were lynched by vigilante squads, and they earned Australians a vile reputation in California.

A few years later the Californians had their revenge by exporting to Australia a lady called Lola Montez. In California she'd made a name by living with a pet bear, throwing her husbands down the stairs, and horsewhipping editors who criticised her appalling spider dance. She didn't forget these tricks in Australia.

In November 1850, a man with a more important bag of tricks waited on the San Francisco wharves to catch a ship back to Australia. He was about to change the history of Australia as dramatically as Marshall had changed the history of America, and at much greater profit to himself. His name was Edward Hammond Hargraves.

Edward Hammond Hargraves

Born in England, Hargraves had first come to Australia as a cabin boy on the ship of one Captain Lister. He had grown into a mountain of flesh, six foot three and twenty stone. He'd failed at a variety of occupations before he joined the gold rush to California. Hargraves was not an energetic digger and he'd won little gold in California. But now he was returning to Australia with something just as valuable—knowledge. He knew there was gold in Australia, because he had heard of the finds by the shepherd, McGregor. And he knew how to get it out of the ground, with techniques that were as yet unknown in Australia. Hargraves wrote:

> It was with an anxious heart that I again landed at Sydney in the month of January, 1851. On my passage thither and immediately on my arrival, I made known to my friends and companions my confident expectations on the subject. One and all however derided me and treated my views and opinions as those of a madman. Still undaunted, on the 5th of February I set out from Sydney on horseback alone to cross the Blue Mountains.

21

The Blue Mountains

Hargraves was long on confidence but he was short of money—he'd had to raise a loan to get his horse—and he was short of time. Other diggers were returning from California, and they knew, like him, that gold had been found at Wellington. Hargraves was on his way there but a chance encounter directed him to Guyong, between Bathurst and Orange.

Hargraves had hopes of staying overnight with the Honourable Thomas Icely of Coombing Park, near Carcoar. But Icely was on his way to Sydney to fight a court case, and he met Hargraves on the road. Perhaps the mention of Wellington prompted him to advise Hargraves to put up at an inn called 'The Wellington Inn' at Guyong. It was the luckiest chance in Hargraves' life.

The historic moment...
Under the eyes of John
Lister, Hargraves pans the
first gold at Lewis Ponds
Creek

The inn was kept by Mrs Lister, widow of the ship's captain who'd once hired Hargraves as a cabin boy. Her son, John Hardman Australia Lister, knew the district well and had found samples of quartz which were displayed on a mantelpiece at the inn. In response to some very interested enquiries, Lister took Hargraves down the Lewis Ponds Creek. Hargraves had spent a couple of days there in 1835, looking for lost bullocks, and he later claimed that he'd remembered the country well.

After travelling a distance of about fifteen miles, I found myself in the country that I was so anxiously longing to behold again. My recollection of it had not deceived me. The resemblance of its formation to that of California could not be doubted or mistaken. I felt myself surrounded by gold, and with tremulous anxiety panted for the moment of trial when my magician's wand should transform this trackless wilderness into a region of countless wealth.

Hargraves' account of the gold discovery, written several years later, implied that he always knew exactly where he was heading. In fact it was John Lister who guided Hargraves to a waterhole on Lewis Ponds Creek, and who provided the packhorse, the food and the equipment Hargraves asked for—a tin dish, a pick and a trowel. But it was Hargraves who knew how to use the equipment. This was his priceless knowledge from California.

> My guide went for water to drink and after making a hasty repast, I told him that we were now in the gold fields, and that the gold was under his feet as he went to fetch the water for our dinner. He stared with incredulous amazement and on my telling him that I would now find some gold, watched my movements with the most intense interest. My own excitement, probably, was far more intense than his. I took the pick, and scratched the gravel off a schistose dyke, which ran across the creek at right angles with its side, and with the trowel I dug a panful of earth, which I washed in the waterhole. The first trial produced a little piece of gold. 'Here it is!' I exclaimed, and I then washed five panfuls in succession, obtaining gold from all but one.

What Hargraves got was five specks of gold, hardly visible to the naked eye. It was the only gold he ever dug out of Australian earth. But it was the first time gold dust had ever been panned in Australia, and it was enough to provoke oratory never heard before at Lewis Ponds Creek.

> This is a memorable day in the history of New South Wales. I shall be a baronet, you will be knighted, and my old horse will be stuffed, put into a glass case, and sent to the British Museum!

Hargraves never became a baronet, although he tried very hard. Lister was never knighted, although he believed Hargraves' promise at the time. And the old horse was never literally stuffed. It should have been, after carting Hargraves' bulk across the country. But Hargraves was right about one thing. February 12, 1851, was indeed a memorable day and it altered the course of the country.

Australia had already changed from its old role as a convict colony. By 1851 it was a country of 400 000 people, most of them free. Sydney was a considerable city. A native Australian character was emerging, and democratic

Early Sydney

institutions were on the way. But economically Australia was in the doldrums, just as America had been when it was rescued from depression by the Californian gold strike.

It was in fact the Californian rush which altered Australian attitudes. Governor Fitzroy was alarmed by the loss of able-bodied emigrants to California, and he employed a government geologist to investigate Australia's mineral prospects. But the Governor was still cautious. He wanted evidence of payable gold mines, rich enough to compensate for the disruption they might cause in the country.

When Hargraves came to Sydney with his five specks of gold and claimed a reward, the Governor was not convinced. This was not enough. He said that any reward would depend on Hargraves revealing the location of a payable goldfield. It was bad news for Hargraves. He'd gambled everything on making the first claim on the Government for a reward. But he hadn't dug enough, and one thing he'd learnt in California was that gold digging was hard work. Hargraves himself admitted:

It had never been my intention, in connection with this discovery, to work for gold. My only desire was

25

Above: *The junction of Summerhill Creek and Lewis Ponds Creek, Ophir*
Opposite: *A gold cradle*

to make the discovery, and rely on the Government and the country for my reward.

Meanwhile, back at the creek near Guyong, two men *were* working for gold and working hard. They were John Lister and his mate William Tom, from nearby Springfield. William had built a strange device. He told enquirers it was a cage to catch birds on the Canobolas Mountain, and every bird would be worth a pound. In fact, it was another trick that Hargraves had brought back from California. He'd shown Lister and Tom how to build it and how to use it before he went to Sydney to stake his claim for a reward. It was a cradle, and it was destined to rock the golden baby at Australia's first goldfield.

The principle was simple enough. The dirt and gravel were shovelled into the cradle, followed by buckets of water. The rocking action spilt the rubbish out of the cradle. The gold, being heavier, was caught by the riffles in the cradle, and could be panned off later.

27

William Tom with nugget and cradle

The problem was to find gold-bearing gravel. Lister and Tom did just that on April 7, 1851, at the junction of Lewis Ponds and Summerhill Creek. They washed four ounces of gold, worth more than twelve pounds. This was enough to pay a miner's wage for several months. It was a payable goldfield.

Lister and Tom wrote and told Hargraves the news, and Hargraves was galvanised into action. He immediately told the government the location of the goldfield and arranged to take the Government geologist there. But first he galloped up and got the four ounces of gold from Lister and Tom. He flashed it around in Bathurst and then sent it to the Governor. He gave public lectures, he planted newspaper stories, he told everyone about it. He did his best to start a gold rush, and he succeeded brilliantly. He also succeeded in starting an argument which has lingered on in Australia to this day.

Hargraves named the junction of Lewis Ponds and Summerhill Creek, Ophir—the name the Bible gave to the fabulous goldmines of King Solomon. It was typical of Hargraves' quick intelligence and flair for publicity. But in all his publicity there was little mention of Lister and Tom. They'd found the gold at Ophir, but they became the forgotten men of Australian history.

Hargraves got all the glory and almost all the rewards. He was feted everywhere, given silver tea services and gold cups and watches, more than twelve thousand pounds from the Colonial Governments, and a lucrative Crown Commission to find more gold. He didn't find another speck of gold before he retired in splendour to Norahville, which perhaps indicates that he was lucky the first time. There's no doubt he deserved a reward. He introduced the dish and the cradle from California, he started the gold rush, and he knew just how to play his cards.

However, when Hargraves was running out of cards, it was Lister and Tom who handed him the ace, by telling him they'd found payable gold at Ophir and letting him get the gold which he used to start the rush. They did it, they said, because they were all partners and Hargraves promised them all the rewards would be shared.

Hargraves denied to the end of his life that there had ever been any partnership agreement. The following statements, given by the three parties in evidence to the subsequent Parliamentary enquiries, show how greatly they differed on this point.

Tom: 'The understanding was that we were to have a fair representation to the Government. We would not otherwise have given him the gold. That was the understanding. I cannot say what words were used, we trusted to his honour.'

Hargraves: 'It was not an agreement, but only a verbal arrangement. I was never connected with them. They were connected with me for their own good. Tom and Lister knew no more about making a cradle than a watch, and laughed at the idea.'

Tom: 'Yes, he is fully entitled to the credit of having made us acquainted with the mode of extracting the

Above: *Hargraves' house, Norahville*
Opposite: *The four ounces of gold*

gold from the soil.'

Lister: 'He said he wished to prove that it was a workable goldfield. We at once gave him the four ounces of gold . . .'

Hargraves: 'I never had gold placed by them in my possession. I bought the gold and paid for it. The finding of this four ounces of gold did not in any way influence my proceedings.'

Lister: 'One rub of an old file would take more gold off a sovereign than Mr. Hargraves got altogether.'

Tom: 'While in the Bathurst district, Hargraves never dug a hole a foot deep.'

Hargraves: 'I never stopped to dig for gold. I had seen quite enough of the country and hurried to Sydney to make my arrangements with the Government and to register my claim.'

Lister: 'He wished to hoodwink the Government, to

deceive the public, and bamboozle us, in all of which he has tolerably well succeeded.'

The Tom family of Springfield, with the Listers, petitioned, wrote, argued and agitated throughout half a century and three Parliamentary enquiries to get justice for their claims, and their descendants still hold their cause dear. Mrs Beth Pearce, the great grand-daughter of William Tom, acknowledges that Hargraves taught Lister and Tom the use of the dish and cradle, but says he then behaved like an utter bounder. He concealed his intentions from his partners and used their gold to get the rewards and the glory which he refused to share with them.

From the house at Norahville on the New South Wales central coast, which he built from his reward money, Hargraves spent the rest of his life defending his reputation and his honour—and *his* descendants are still involved in the fight. His great grand-daughter, Mrs Edie Foley, who now occupies the house, says quite simply that Hargraves was a great man, that it was his initiative and vision which changed Australian history, and that he deserves every bit of his fame.

So a struggle that began at Ophir in 1851 continues to this day. The New South Wales Parliament, which gave Hargraves ten thousand pounds, gave Lister and the Toms one thousand between them—after they'd petitioned—and that's all they ever got. But it wasn't just a fight for money. It was a fight for a place in history. And a Parliamentary enquiry, forty years after the discovery, gave that place to Lister and Tom. Its verdict was the one recorded on the monument at Ophir in 1923. Edward Hargraves introduced the dish and the cradle from California, and taught their use. John Lister and William Tom discovered the first payable gold in Australia. That is not what generations of Australian school children learned from their history books, in which Edward Hargraves was given the sole credit for the discovery of gold. But it was the opinion of the first Government official on the spot at Ophir, Commissioner Charles Green. Green reported:

No doubt Hargraves showed these young men how to obtain the gold and without his assistance they in all probability could not have found it but I believe they were the actual finders of gold in sufficient quantities to pay, and they spent a good deal of time and money in the search.

Governor Fitzroy

He might have added that they paid Hargraves' expenses, so they had reason to believe they were partners with him. But it was a classic case of not getting it down in writing. Lister and Tom could produce no document of agreement with Hargraves. In the circumstances, they could have taken their four ounces of gold to Sydney without telling Hargraves, and claimed a reward for themselves. But they were not the men to take such a course.

Meanwhile at Ophir Commissioner Green was too busy to speculate about such matters. He was trying to control something Australia had never experienced—a gold rush. The rush was a direct result of a public lecture given in Bathurst by Hargraves as soon as he obtained Lister's and Tom's gold. The *Bathurst Free Press* reported:

Discovery of an extensive gold field

Mr. Hargraves states as the result of his observations that from the foot of the Big Hill to a considerable distance below Wellington on the Macquarie is one vast Gold field; that he has actually discovered the precious metal in numberless places; that he has established a company of nine working miners who are now actively employed, digging at a point of the Summer Hill Creek near its junction with the Macquarie, about 50 miles from Bathurst and 30 from Guyong. Ophir is the name given to these diggings. Several samples of fine Gold were shown to the Company by Mr. Hargraves, weighing in all about four ounces . . .

The morning this report appeared, May 10, 1851, numerous parties left Bathurst on horseback for the diggings. Within a week, there were six hundred men toiling furiously at Ophir. The Government geologist, Samuel Stutchbury, arrived on the scene and soon informed Governor Fitzroy that the gold strike was no mirage.

Gold has been obtained in considerable quantity, many persons with merely a tin dish or other inefficient apparatus having obtained one to two ounces per day. I have no doubt of gold being found over a vast extent of country. I fear unless something is done very quickly that much confusion will arise . . . Excuse this being written in pencil, as there is no ink yet in this city of Ophir.

Back in Sydney, Governor Fitzroy was not prepared for a

gold rush which Hargraves had started before there were any regulations. But he reacted quickly and issued proclamations that all gold legally belonged to the Crown. However, the diggers could get it if they paid a licence fee of thirty shillings a month. In other words, it was to be 'Finders Keepers'—for a price.

This licence fee was going to cause a lot of trouble later. The diggers would say it was too much, especially for the unlucky ones. But the Government had its reasons. It wanted to extract some revenue from the gold and finance a system of law and order on the diggings. And it particularly wanted to discourage every shepherd and tradesman and labourer from downing tools and rushing away for gold. The conservative class, the squatters and the employers, feared that gold would wreck the system. The *Sydney Morning Herald* lamented:

It appears that this colony is to be cursed with a gold-digging mania. Many persons are going to dig for gold who are wholly unfit for such work; men who would hesitate to walk the length of George Street in a shower of rain. What can be the result of such reckless conduct but that which happened in California—ruin, misery, disease, death.

The People's Advocate which represented the radical point of view was simultaneously excited and troubled:

GOLD! GOLD! GOLD!

Never before was there such a glorious opportunity of upsetting, and for ever, the infamous oligarchical system which in this colony has too long tyrannised over the people. But these regulations are extremely harsh, and show that the Government are even yet disposed to favour the squatters to the utmost of their power.

Elsewhere the Sydney press was full of curious reports and advertisements:

'Spring-carts for the Diggings!'

'Quicksilver for amalgamating Gold-Soil!'

'Waterproof tents for the El Dorado!'

'Single and Double Guns and Pistols—For Self-Defence!'

'The New Rush', ST Gill

'Chocolate. Every miner should provide himself with Peek Co's superior Flake Chocolate!'

'Laver & Co's Ophir cordial. No-one who values his health or comfort should proceed to the Gold Field without a supply!'

'As the colony is now advancing to a state of unprecedented richness, and the empire of Australia will yet rival the age called The Golden, Leopold Morgan & Co. offer their recently compounded cordial—the elixir of life—which will expand the benumbed veins of the Gold washers!'

The word 'mad' cropped up frequently in the reports of the time:

Sydney is going stark, staring mad. GOLD! GOLD!

Early diggers at Ophir

GOLD! is the one and only topic from the merchant down to the chimney sweep. Little else is thought of or talked about. Labourers and tradesmen are striking for wages and leaving in all directions. Sailors are deserting their ships, and young men in good situations giving notice, or throwing up employment at once.

A participant in these first days of excitement recalled later:

Sydney *was* mad. You could not converse with any man in town except on that one topic, gold. You went to the doctor and told him you were ill; he would feel your pulse and ask you, not if you had pains in the head or anywhere else—but if you had heard the last accounts from the mines!

Boastful balladeers asserted that the Ophir gold strike would put the Yankees in the shade:

Hurrah for the diggings! The cry gathers strength, boys
And fortune now smiles on the gallant and bold
The good time long promised is coming at length, boys
Then away—pick and cradle—to gather the gold!

Hurrah for the diggings! to Bathurst away, boys,
California is beaten, the Yankees outdone,
Their famed El Dorado has now had its day, boys,
Tis time that Australia should share in the fun!

Take time by the forelock, ye doubters and scoffers,
Seize fortune when near without doubt or delay,
Be off to the gold mines and see what it offers,
Tis an Ophir that will not turn up every day!

At Circular Quay ships lay empty as outward-bound passengers jumped off again to join the rush. Businesses closed down as their staff grabbed their hats and deserted to the goldfields. Sporting events were called off, public meetings were abandoned, even the traditional Queen's Birthday Ball was cancelled. Schools were closed down, because the teachers had gone off to take lessons in gold-digging.

Few people were left in town to read the editorial moanings of Granny *Herald*:

As it appears to be impossible to avoid the trial the colony has to go through, it must be met boldly, although we fear it will be attended by the ruin of thousands. It becomes the duty of every sober-minded man in the community to look the danger calmly but fully in the face. Let us hope that the treasure does not exist in large quantities, and that experience will soon convince the people that the ordinary pursuits of industry are the safest and the best.

Governor Fitzroy wrote to England that a very great excitement was engrossing and unhinging the minds of all classes, and that he had no more chance of stopping the rush than of stopping the ocean tides. Along the Parramatta Road, a great flood of humanity poured westward. Colonel Mundy described this extraordinary procession:

I counted nearly sixty drays and carts, heavily laden, proceeding westward with tents, rockers, flour, tea, mining tools—each accompanied by from four to eight men, half of whom bore firearms. Many I thought would never return. They must have thrown

*'Off to the Rush',
(Hatherall)*

all they possessed into the adventure, for most of their equipments were quite new—good stout horses, harness fresh out of the saddler's hands, gay-coloured woollen shirts, and comforters and Californian sombreros of every hue and shape. It was a strange sight—a strange jumble of images!

At the Nepean River crossing, Penrith experienced the first traffic jam, as dozens of drays and thousands of people waited to get across. Amongst them were gentlemen on fine horses, kilted Scotsmen led by pipers, runaway sailors and servants, blind men, lame men and poor men with their worldly goods in wheelbarrows and their children harnessed to their backs. Many had little chance of success, but also little to lose. Up at Carcoar, the Honourable Thomas Icely, the squire of Coombing Park, was watching the rush go by and perhaps regretting that

'Early Goldfields', ST Gill

he'd ever told Edward Hargraves how to get to the Guyong Inn. He wrote in dismay to Sydney:

> I apprehend great danger. I have removed my plate and other valuables and do not intend to reside in my house. I fear that my own and all other stores along the line of road will be pillaged, and there are no means of police communication.

A weird procession struggled across the Blue Mountains and down to the Macquarie River crossing between Kelso and Bathurst. There were people who'd never been seen west of the ranges—hurdy gurdy men, Punch and Judy men, Sydney exquisites with shining spurs and kid gloves and opera ties, reeking of hair oil and eau de cologne. It was reported that two Parramatta doctors had arrived with a portable hospital—a dozen folded tents, twenty-five collapsible stretchers and fifty coffins filled with flour. The

The Turon Widow ('Goodbye, my love, goodbye')

price of flour and all necessities had magically doubled, and the goldfields crowd included plenty of Van Diemonian desperadoes bristling with guns and bowie knives. So the good doctors looked like pulling the double jackpot with their coffins.

The *Bathurst Free Press*, whose story had started the gold rush, watched with mingled excitement and fear. It reported that the mania had seized all classes. The farmers were leaving their ploughs, and nothing was talked of, thought of, or dreamed of but gold. There were few single men left in Bathurst, the married ones only stayed because they had to, and the newspaper was thinking of migrating to the diggings too. Like the Sydney press, it spoke of 'gold fever' and 'madness':

A complete mental madness appears to have seized almost every member of the community and there has been a universal rush to the diggings. The people of all trades, callings and pursuits were quickly transformed into miners, and many a hand which had been trained to kid gloves, or accustomed to wield nothing heavier than the grey goose-quill, became nervous to clutch the pick and crowbar or rock the cradle at our infant mines.

Ophir was now a canvas city of two thousand diggers, and the banks of the Summerhill Creek were being torn apart by the frenzied miners. The first Gold Commissioner, John Hardy, was on the field issuing licences, marking out claims and settling disputes. At this stage there was little resistance to the licence fee. Hardy was a sensible man who didn't press the diggers too hard. And, besides, they were getting good gold—ten thousand pounds' worth in the first week.

The life was uncomfortable, the work hard, and the diggings so crowded together that a man could hit his neighbour with the swing of his pick and sometimes did. But in late May the pressure on Ophir was relieved by a new rush. Gold had been found on the nearby Turon River.

> *Goodbye, my love, goodbye,*
> *My cradle's on the dray,*
> *To rock out gold for thee, love,*
> *To the Turon I must away.*

The Turon field was bigger and richer than Ophir, and its capital was given the name Sofala after the African territory where King Solomon's legendary Ophir mine was thought to be located.

Brucedale, at Peel near Bathurst, was the homestead of the Suttor family, pioneer settlers. They were not related to the American Captain Sutter, but like him, they feared the disruption that gold would cause to their established way of life. From her house on the hill, Charlotte Suttor watched the weird parade passing along the gold road to the Turon, and wrote in her diary:

26th May. GOLD, GOLD. The God of mammon has surely unfurled his banner here and hundreds are flocking to the standard. Nothing else seems to occupy people's minds. Such a complete revolution in its affairs never came over a country in the same space of time.

Charlotte Suttor complained that her house had become like a hotel, but a few weeks later she was out in the paddocks herself looking at rocks. How could anyone resist the gold mania? Her brother-in-law, Dr Kerr, had an Aboriginal shepherd who'd hacked at a quartz outcrop with a tomahawk and found it chockful of gold. He told Dr Kerr who raced to the spot and broke up the rock so he could shift it. This was unfortunate, since he was breaking up the biggest mass of quartz gold yet found in the world. Dr Kerr stuffed the broken rock in his saddlebags, and stored it overnight in the Suttors' cupboard at Brucedale. When he got it to Bathurst, it was found to contain over a hundred pounds' weight of gold. In modern values, it was worth nearly half a million dollars. This time the *Bathurst Free Press* went right off the scale:

> Bathurst is mad again! The delirium of golden fever has returned with increased intensity. Men meet together, stare stupidly at each other, talk incoherent nonsense, and wonder what will happen next. Everybody has a hundred times seen a hundred-weight of flour; a hundred-weight of sugar or potatoes is an every-day fact, but a hundred-weight of gold is a phrase scarcely known in the English language.

In 1851, 2000 gold licences were issued at Ophir, 1000 at Meroo River, 9000 at the Turon. The Turon became the major goldfield of New South Wales. From Sofala to Tambaroora, the ground was ripped up by diggers and rich rewards were won. Wealthy diggers from the Turon, 'Tambaroora Johnnies', became the subject of Sydney music hall songs.

> *It was just about a year ago, as near as I can guess,*
> *When I left dear old Sydney Town in trouble and distress.*
> *My friends and sweetheart slighted me and gave me turnips cold,*
> *Until a voice cried in my ear, 'Try Tambaroora gold!'*
>
> *I'd not been long upon the fields before I got a job,*
> *And worked six months for wages with a chap named Dusty Bob.*
> *With that a claim I purchased, and while turning up the mould,*
> *My pile I soon created with bright Tambaroora gold.*
>
> *Then I came back to Sydney Town, a regular dashing swell,*
> *And strange to say my previous friends all seemed to*

Moore's Wharf, Sydney

wish me well.
They lowly bowed and touched their hats as up the
street I strolled;
But thinks I, they don't want Johnny but his Tam-
baroora gold!

From Moore's Wharf on the Sydney Rocks, the first ship-
ment of Australian gold left for England in 1851. It was valued at £81 000, but its symbolic value was much greater
than that, because it was about to change forever the overseas image of the former convict colony, and to turn Australia from a country almost nobody wanted to go to, into
a country everyone wanted to go to.

Gold also changed the colonials' image of themselves,
and they started to beat the drum about their new El
Dorado. *The People's Advocate* thought it was definitely
one in the eye for Old England:

A high and noble destiny awaits the long despised
Australia, and she must now be treated by her
haughty mistress, not as a child, but as an equal. In
every point a great change must be, or Australia will
know how to vindicate her *rights.*

Even the *Sydney Morning Herald* abandoned gloom, and
forecast:

Population and wealth will flow in upon us in copi-
ous, rapid and continuous streams.

Meanwhile in Melbourne the merchants and employers
were gnashing their teeth. Just as the Port Phillip district
was becoming the self-governing colony of Victoria, half
the workmen were rushing off to New South Wales to look

for gold. And so on June 11, 1851, the *Port Phillip Gazette* carried this notice:

TWO HUNDRED GUINEAS REWARD

The committee appointed by the general meeting held in Melbourne on the 9th instant, is now prepared to offer a reward of

TWO HUNDRED GUINEAS

to any person or persons who shall discover to them a

GOLD MINE

or **DEPOSIT** within 200 miles of Melbourne capable of being worked to advantage, this amount to be independent of any reward the Government may be disposed to grant.

WILLIAM NICHOLSON, MAYOR
CHAIRMAN

The committee didn't have to wait long. Within a month there were numerous claimants for the reward, and gold rushes were under way at Warrandyte, east of Melbourne, and Clunes to the north-west. Clunes was the major find and the man responsible was James Esmond.

Happy Jim Esmond was a returned Californian like Hargraves. In fact he came back to Australia on the same ship, and that wasn't the only similarity between the gold strikes at Ophir and at Clunes. As in New South Wales, gold had been found in Victoria before 1851. Ten miles west of Clunes at Amherst a shepherd boy named Chapman got thirty-eight ounces of gold in 1849. That was ten times more than the gold that started the Ophir rush, but somehow nothing came of it. Californian experience was the winning trick. The rewards for payable gold went to men who knew how to make it pay.

Victoria soon repaid the gold search in returns that put New South Wales in the shade. A succession of gold rushes followed Clunes—Buninyong in August, Ballarat in September, Castlemaine in October, Bendigo in December of 1851. Those remarkable names, Ballarat and Bendigo, were soon to ring around the world, making golden music in men's ears. Victoria was about to eclipse California, and Australia was on the high road to fortune.

Eureka

Arrival of the first gold escort at Melbourne

The news of the gold discoveries of 1851 burst on Victoria like a bomb. In the countryside, stock were left to die and crops were left to rot as the farm labourers rushed away to the goldfields. The first effects on Melbourne were just as drastic. Whole streets were deserted and some suburbs were left without a single able-bodied male. The police force deserted down to the last man. The staff of Mr Hoddle, the surveyor, after witnessing from their office windows the arrival of the first gold escort in Melbourne, left for the goldfields the next morning.

Bishop Perry displayed a notice imploring his stonemasons for the love of God and thirty shillings a day, to keep on building his Anglican church. But love of gold proved more powerful than love of God, and the stonemasons absconded.

Business came to a standstill. The shopkeepers, their staff and their customers dropped everything and headed up country for gold. They were soon to be followed by a much bigger swarm of newcomers. As the news reached the world that folks in Australia were picking up lumps of gold, a rush began that was to put California in the shade, triple Australia's population in ten years, from 400 000 to 1 168 000 and produce in that decade one hundred and twenty-four million pounds' worth of gold.

'To Emigrants'

From Britain and Ireland alone, half a million emigrants set sail on the long voyage to Australia. They included all manner of people—sculptors and blacksmiths, drapers and poets, clergymen, farmers and soldiers of fortune. The emigrants paid fifteen pounds for steerage class, fifty pounds for a cabin, and all they got was space on the ship—they had to provide beds, dishes, knives and forks.

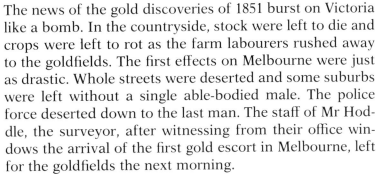

45

Guidebooks advised them to take a great variety of goods, many of them ridiculous. The most practical advice was to pack some food, as the ship's provisions were usually terrible. One passenger confided to his diary:

Our first meal at sea was at least half bone, and as hard to cut as a cable. It was not only hard and dreadfully salt, but very bad. One of the passengers told me he saw the casks carefully covered over directly the inspector came on board at Gravesend. I myself saw some salt beef or horse quite green and stinking. I have no doubt if this goes on we shall have some desperate work. There are enough mutinous fellows on board who will not quietly submit to this filthy offal for food, after they have paid full price for passage-money.

For some passengers, the question of food was irrelevant, because they were sick all the way from the Bay of Biscay to Bass Strait.

> *Left Plymouth one day in July*
> *And soon was on the ocean*
> *That I should 'scape sea sickness*
> *I had a curious notion*
> *All the while that it was calm*
> *I felt quite gay and frisky*
> *But Oh! how pale and ill I looked*
> *When on the Bay of Biscay . . .*

Thus Charles Thatcher, the English music hall entertainer who became the darling of the goldfields, joked about his voyage to Australia. Many passengers found the experience less amusing. The journey by sailing ship from Europe to Melbourne in the 1850s took four or five months. It was cramped and uncomfortable, often rough and always tedious. The passengers had no diversions except a few concerts they organised themselves, or the occasional fight, or the excitement of catching a shark. Yet hundreds of thousands of our ancestors undertook this voyage and most of them paid their own way. They were buoyed up by hope.

They had read of Australia as the promised land where in one day a man might pick up two pounds of gold before dinner. When they arrived in Port Phillip Bay, with perhaps only pickles and bilge water left of their provisions, they besieged the pilot to ask if there was still enough gold left for them. In Port Phillip Bay, they joined a host of

Goldrush fleet in Hobson's Bay, Melbourne

other ships from all nations.

Melbourne was only twenty-five years old, and still fairly primitive, but as the Italian digger Rafaello Carboni found, inflation was well advanced:

> As an old European traveller I had set apart a few coppers for the poor at my landing. My care for the poor would have less disappointed me, if I had prepared myself against falling in the clutches of a shoal of land-sharks, who swarmed at that time the Yarra Yarra wharfs. Five pounds for landing my luggage! Rapacity in Australia is the Alpha and Omega. Yet there were no poor! a grand reflection for the serious.

It was a time of tremendous optimism, and everyone was infected by it. Aspiring diggers from every quarter of the globe huddled in the canvas town south of the Yarra and prepared to strike out for the goldfields. They were a motley crew, and so were the locals of Melbourne, but they all had at least one thing in common. They were afflicted by a disease whose alarming symptoms had now become front page news.

GOLD FEVER

A medical friend informs us that the prevailing epidemic resembles ordinary fever at its commencement, as the premonitory symptoms are restlessness, anxiety, and a disinclination to follow one's ordinary avocations.

During the first stages of the attack a sufferer may be known by an unshorn beard, a dirty face, and an embryo bandit appearance.

Gold ships approaching Melbourne

As the disease advances, the patient sticks a short pipe in his mouth, and assumes a red shirt and a pair of moleskin trousers.

If the symptoms are unchecked by a rise in his salary, all objects he views appear of a golden hue—excitement terminates in delirium—one morn we miss him from the custom'd spot—and the answer to all the anxious inquiries of his friends, is that he was last seen on a loaded bullock dray, provided with a straw mattress, a tin pannikin, a shovel and a cradle.

The gold fever was spurred on by a succession of discoveries, each apparently richer than the last. The first rushes to Clunes and Warrandyte in July 1851 were followed by tremendous new finds at Buninyong, Ballarat, Castlemaine and Bendigo. By December they had produced nine million pounds' worth of gold. The struggling pastoral district of Port Phillip had been transformed in one remarkable year into Victoria the Golden. It seemed there was no end to the wealth of this lucky colony. The excitement of the people was echoed and even egged on by the Melbourne press.

The *Argus* bellowed: 'Eureka! We have gold—gold in abundance!' And an *Argus* correspondent told of amazing scenes in Geelong:

The whole town of Geelong is in hysterics. Gentlemen foaming at the mouth, ladies fainting, children throw-

ing somersets, and all on account of the extraordinary
news from Buninyong.

In 1851 Victoria became not just a new colony, but a new
kind of society. The diggers spoke a new tongue. They
talked of washing and cradling and puddling, of whips and
whims and windlasses. They sported a digger's uniform,
straw and cabbagetree hats, blue and red flannel shirts,
moleskin trousers and tough boots. They tasted a new kind
of life, a gypsy life, tramping from field to field, Ballarat
today, Bendigo tomorrow.

Fortune favoured the lucky, but it also favoured the
hardworking, resolute and brawny digger. There were no
favourites in the race for gold, no handicaps of breeding
or social connections. There was a prospect of freedom
and independence for people who had never enjoyed these
luxuries. It was a time of high hopes for the immigrant and
the native-born Australian. Poets penned odes:

> To man, to progress, and to all
> The free things, nobly free
> Of which their loved Australia shall
> The golden cradle be.

Charles Thatcher, in his finest gold ballad 'Look Out
Below' (or 'Song of Ballarat') voiced the feelings of men
at a vital moment in their lives, when they were transfer-
ring their loyalties from an old country to a new country:

> A young man left his native shores
> For trade was bad at home
> To seek his fortune in this land
> He crossed the briny foam.
> And when he went to Ballarat
> It put him in a glow
> To hear the sound of the windlass
> And the cry 'Look Out Below'.

> Wherever he turned his wandering eyes
> Great wealth he did behold
> And peace and plenty hand in hand
> By the magic power of gold.
> Quoth he, as I am young and strong
> To the diggings I will go
> For I like the sound of the windlass
> And the cry 'Look Out Below'.

> Among the rest he took his chance
> And his luck at first was vile

Early diggings

But he still resolved to persevere
And at length he made his pile.
So says he, I'll take my passage
And home again I'll go
And I'll say farewell to the windlass
And the cry 'Look Out Below'.

Arrived in London once again
His gold he freely spent
And into every gaiety
And dissipation went.
But pleasure if prolonged too much
Oft causes pain, you know,
And he missed the sound of the windlass
And the cry 'Look Out Below'.

And thus he reasoned with himself
Oh, why did I return
For the digger's independent life
I now begin to yearn
Here purse proud lords the poor oppress
But there it is not so
Give me the sound of the windlass
And the cry 'Look Out Below'.

So he started for this land again
With a charming little wife
And he finds there's nothing comes up to
A jolly digger's life
Ask him if he'll go back again
He'll quickly answer, No,
For he loves the sound of the windlass
And the cry 'Look Out Below'.

For many centuries before the diggers came, other nomadic tribes had roamed the hills and plains of Victoria. The Aboriginals had enjoyed the hunting rights to these territories for thousands of years. They were displaced and dispossessed in less than twenty years by the squatters. In the 1830s these pioneering pastoralists with their shepherds and their flocks spread out across Victoria and occupied huge tracts of land.

Theirs was the wool that earned Victoria's income. Theirs was the voice that counted most with Victoria's governors. With the discovery of gold, and the arrival of a multitude of strangers on their doorstep, the squatters felt themselves under siege, just as the Aboriginals had been from them. Men like the Reverend Joseph Docker, in his rural seat of Bontharambo, weren't sure what to make of the gold rush, or how to handle it.

Following Major Mitchell's explorations of Victoria, and his glowing reports of 'Australia Felix', Docker had overlanded from Sydney to the Ovens River in 1838, bringing with him his family, a retinue of servants and 3000 sheep. He had managed to weather the depression of the 1840s, when world prices for wool collapsed. By the 1850s his flocks had greatly increased, but his vast holdings were still unfenced, and he relied entirely on his shepherds to guard his sheep. When gold was discovered at nearby Beechworth, nineteen of his twenty stockmen deserted him. Strange and disreputable characters tramped in droves across his property, which he did not own, but only held under the precarious annual licence of a squatter.

Docker, like many squatters, fancied that ruin stared him in the face. It was only gradually that his fears faded, with the realisation that the diggers wanted meat and would pay handsomely for it—so handsomely that he was able to buy the freehold of his run and erect his magnificent Bontharambo homestead.

When the gold rushes began, there were no Victorian settlements of any importance outside Melbourne, Geelong and Buninyong, and the interior of the country was practically virgin bush. The diggers soon changed the appearance of the country.

> We have begun to destroy the beauty of this creek. It will no longer run clear between its banks, covered with wattles and tea-trees. A little while, and its whole course will exhibit nothing but nakedness, and heaps of gravel and mud. We diggers are horribly destructive of the picturesque.

But there were other realities the digger could not change, like the nature of the work. Very few could pick up lumps of gold. Most had to dig for it, and that was no fun.

> It's only the first blister that hurts. That blister, I can tell you, is terrible, immense; it is as big as the two hands that it invades, swells and deforms. It really hurts. The pain starts at the finger tips, and goes under the nails and moves up as far as the shoulders. I am not sure whether it is the same pain that extends from the shoulders along the spinal column, sticking needles in between the vertebrae, torturing you to such an extent that it is sometimes impossible to stand up, so that for a time you drag yourself along the ground on all fours. In any case you have a terrible pain in the back also. I shall never forget what sighing and groaning the first week of our sorry initiation cost my partners and me.

And after all the hard work, gold digging was still a gamble. The hole might be a shicer, and the digger might lose. But there were some people who always seemed to win—the squatters who sold their beasts, the butchers, the teamsters, the storekeepers. On the early goldfields they had the diggers at their mercy and they could sink the fangs deep.

A disgruntled Englishman penned this ditty:

*They'll charge yer seven shillings for a pint of mouldy
peas
Six and ninepence farthing for a pound of rotten
cheese
Of going a gold-digging, friends, I think I've had me
fill
May the devil take Australia, I'll live with old John
Bull.
Now my friends take my advice
Never never seek to go
Or you will rue the day, the day
You went out to Australia-o.*

Opposite: *'The Gold
Buyer'*, ST Gill

A visitor to the goldfields reported:

Among the placards which attracted our eyes was one
with immense letters. 'EGGS! EGGS! EGGS! Immense reduction in Eggs! EGGS now only ONE
SHILLING EACH!' They were a few days ago two
shilling each.

And a former digger complained;

*I've come back all skin and bone
From the diggins—oh
And I wish I'd never gone
To the diggins—oh.
Believe me, 'tis no fun
I once weighed fifteen stone
But they brought me down to one
At the diggins—oh.*

The work was thirsty and the life was hard. It was not surprising that the diggers took to the grog with enthusiasm.
But there were no licensed hotels in the early goldfields,
only sly grog tents and shanties. The diggers weren't so
much round the barrel as over it. They had to pay double
for their drinks, but they reckoned that was better than
going dry. A popular music hall ballad celebrated the
rough-and-ready pleasure palaces of the goldfields:

*The grog tent we got tipsy in, on old Bendigo
Was certainly the queerest place it's been my lot to
know
'Twas in the gulley where we worked, and on my
word its true
We could knock out our ounce a day, and ten feet
sinking too
We'd then of course no fine hotels, but thought quite
great, you know*

Coffee Tent & Sly Diggers Bread

That grog tent we got tipsy in, on old Bendigo
That grog tent we got tipsy in, on old Bendigo.

It wasn't more than twelve by eight, no window had
or door
The tables, seats, were all bush made and fixed into
the floor
We nobblers drank in pannikins, two shillings for
them paid
For to knock down a note or two, we then were not
afraid
The landlady was pretty and the chaps all flocked you
know
The grog tent we got tipsy in, on old Bendigo
The grog tent we got tipsy in, on old Bendigo.

Gold wasn't too easy to get, but it was always easy to spend. The remoteness of the early diggings, the primitive

Left: *'Coffee Tent and "Sly Grog" shop—Diggers Breakfast', ST Gill*
Right: *The Vandemonian cartoon*

roads and the difficulties of transport bumped the price of goods sky high. And there were other ways to lose your gold. The goldfields were full of desperate characters. Prominent amongst them were the ex-convicts who swarmed across the Bass Strait from Tasmania—the dread Van Diemonians.

A cartoon of the day depicted one of them boasting:

> I'm a bloody Vandemonian. I served my bloody time like a bloody man and can pull my bloody shirt off and show my bloody marks.

The Van Diemonians' bad habits weren't limited to bad language. They found there were easier ways of getting gold than working for it, and many turned thief and bush-ranger. Robberies were common and murders frequent. The guilty parties were seldom caught by the police, and in many cases, the crimes went undetected. Charles Joseph Latrobe, the Governor of Victoria at the outbreak of the rush, himself wrote:

'Butcher's Shamble',
ST Gill

Many a murder takes place, of the existence of which no evidence will ever transpire or record exist.

In these lawless conditions, the diggers often formed kangaroo courts, or 'roll-ups', and dealt out their own rough justice. Thieves were flogged and in some cases lynched, and many diggers carried guns to protect their winnings.

Lord Robert Cecil visited the Victorian goldfields as a young man, and judged them remarkably peaceful and law-abiding. But Lord Robert, who was later to be Prime Minister of England, may have been wearing his political blinkers at the time. Other eye-witnesses described the goldfields as a violent and frightening society. Mrs Ellen Clacy, an astute English observer, reported:

Murder here—murder there—revolvers cracking—blunderbusses bombing—rifles going off—balls whistling—a man groaning with a broken leg—another shouting because he couldn't find the way to his hole, and a third equally vociferous because he has tumbled into one.

As for bushrangers, they weren't all out lurking in the bush. Storekeepers and others who bought gold had their own tricks for lightening the digger's purse. The gold buyer

*'Gentleman from the Bush
who is of opinion that he
can take it out of any man
in the Room'*

might insist on weighing the gold in lots of little parcels
instead of in one lot. When he added it all up in a series
of rapid calculations, his mathematics could cost the digger an ounce or two of gold.

Or the buyer could use falsely balanced scales, or have
one pan weighted in his own favour. Unless the digger
insisted on weighing the gold twice, once in each pan, he'd
lose. Or the buyer might insist on inspecting the gold for
quality before he weighed it. He would shake and rub the
gold dust around in a well-greased zinc pan, and some of
it was bound to stick to the sides. The gold buyer might
cultivate very long fingernails. Whenever he stuck them in
the pan, a bit of the gold dust stuck to him. By running
his fingers constantly through his greasy locks he could
make a lot of gold dust stick to him, and become Goldi-
locks or the golden-haired boy, literally.

'The Traps'

The goldfields held lots of traps for young players. In theory there was the protection of law and order in the shape of the goldfields police. But they were the people the diggers called the traps, and regarded as the most dangerous hazard on the Victorian fields. The goldfields police was a raggle taggle band of newcomers. The high officials got their appointments through influence with the Governor and the ranks contained plenty of ex-convicts and doubtful characters whom the diggers regarded as little better than bushrangers in uniforms.

One of their own officers described the traps as 'the most drunken set of men I ever met with'. It could not be claimed that their superiors were of any higher calibre. Some like Inspector Armstrong, nicknamed the Monster', were notorious bullies and crooks. Armstrong carried a riding whip with a heavy brass knob on the end of the handle, and he used it to bash to the ground any digger who looked at him sideways. He was a noted destroyer of grog-tents. On one occasion he ordered his men to set fire

Governor Latrobe

to an Irish widow's tent, knowing that her sleeping children were inside. The wretched woman, who had lost her husband in an accident and had sold sly grog to feed her starving family, screamed, 'For God's sake, sir; spare my tent! Spare my children!'

The traps, for once in their lives, refused to obey an order, and the furious Armstrong sprang from his horse and fired the tent himself. The hysterical woman barely managed to rescue her children, including a baby a few days old, and stood by helplessly as all her worldly goods went up in flames. Armstrong rode away, followed by his men and by the abuse of every digger on the field. They shouted, 'Joe! Joe!'—the term of derision which they reserved for the goldfields police of Charles Joseph Latrobe.

It is little wonder that the diggers grew to hate the traps. Armstrong was dismissed from the force only when public outrage against him could no longer be ignored, and he left Australia with these deathless words: 'I don't mind being turned out, for in these two years, I have cleared £15 000'.

This was a sum equivalent to a million and a half dollars today. How could a man on an official salary of £400 a year, a man who had relentlessly executed the law, acquire such a fortune in two years? The answer was that Armstrong had not relentlessly executed the law. He had destroyed the small sly grog sellers, but permitted the big ones to stay open in return for a share of their profits.

Every digger knew that Armstrong was corrupt, and that he was not the only one. There may have been some honest men in the goldfields police, but the whole system encouraged dishonesty, especially the foolish law which awarded half the fine from every successful prosecution to the policeman who had brought the charge. This strongly encouraged the policeman to commit perjury if necessary to ensure that prosecutions succeeded and he got his money. On the other hand, he could be persuaded not to bring charges if he were offered a bribe worth more than half the fine. Between perjury and bribery, the traps waxed fat, while the whole system of law fell into complete contempt.

There were many hardships on the diggings—the heavy labour; the monotonous diet of mutton, damper and tea; the lack of luxuries and the expense of necessities; the dust, flies and disease; the discomfort of roasting summers and freezing winters spent under canvas.

The Turon River

   With the greatly increased wages which followed the
gold discoveries, many diggers could have made better
money by taking a regular job. But they happened to like
the digger's life. As the writer James Bonwick noted:

   The wild, free and independent life appears the great
   charm. They have no masters. They go where they
   please and work where they will.

These were not the men to be bothered by petty irritations
such as hunger and thirst, but their hackles rose when their
liberty was threatened. As the colonial conservatives remarked with horror, the spirit of democracy was rife
amongst the diggers. Their ranks included English Char-
tists, Scots radicals, Irish rebels and veterans of the 1848
revolutions against the despotic regimes of Europe.

   These diggers regarded the gold licence system, introduced by Governor Fitzroy in New South Wales and
copied by Governor Latrobe in Victoria, as an attack on
them as a class. They did not deny the government's right
to some share of the revenue from the gold industry, but
they reckoned that the licence fee was much too high, and
that the method of collecting it was a scheme of repression

enforced by the government at the urging of the squatters.

Up on the Turon River at Sofala, bitterness between the mining and the squatting interests came close to civil war in February 1853. The diggers' complaint at Sofala was the same as at Ballarat and Bendigo. Thirty shillings a month for a licence was too much, especially as alluvial gold became harder to get. The squatters paid ten pounds a year for a licence to graze their flocks over thousands of acres of Australia's best country. The diggers paid more than that for the right to mine a patch of ground just over two metres square. They had to pay in advance and they had to keep paying whether they found any gold or not. They believed they were being hit with a special tax designed to drive them off the goldfields and into the pastoral work force. And they weren't wrong.

William Charles Wentworth was the chief representative of the great landholders whose profits depended on producing wool cheap and selling it dear to England. The gold rush had made rural labour scarce and expensive. The squatters wanted it abundant and cheap, and Wentworth's Goldfields Act of 1853 was designed to achieve that end. The Act extended their licence fee from working diggers to everyone on the goldfields over the age of fourteen. There were heavy penal clauses for evasion—fines, confiscation of gold and imprisonment.

Anyone who thinks Australia is a conservative country now will find it hard to imagine the mentality of the conservatives of 1853. They regarded democracy as a damnable foreign notion. The main aim of the double tax on aliens was to drive away the Americans and their democratic notions. The government was barking up the wrong tree with this clause. Generally the Americans were respected on the goldfields as hard-working miners who kept their noses out of local politics. But the chief purpose of the Act was to stop the nonsense of people working for themselves as diggers, and get them back into the old social order as servants working for masters. It came as a shock to an industry which had earned Australia millions of pounds and brought it hordes of immigrants in just two years, and reaction on the Turon was nearly revolution.

A roll-up of a thousand diggers at Sofala poured scorn on the New South Wales Government. One of their leaders, Fitzgerald, declared:

> We can and do blame our great mutton men, our woolly-headed lords who toss their heads and cosh up their ugly noses and do all they can by laws and penalties and class legislation to drive us to their prairies to follow the tails of their sheep from morning till night and eat damper and lean beef.

At a second rally they formed a League and resolved not to take out licences. They swore:

> We want no war—above all, no civil war. We want no smoking ruins, nor spilling of Australian blood, shed by Australian arms! We are for peace, but accompanied, it must be, by Liberty!

The Government and the Gold Commissioner replied that the Act would be enforced to the letter. The police barracks at Sofala was reinforced and soldiers were despatched from Sydney.

On Tuesday, February 8, a column of armed diggers started from Mundy Point, four miles east of Sofala. As

'Great Meeting of Gold Diggers', David Tulloch

they marched to the music of fife and drum, they were joined by other diggers, and when they reached Sofala they were 800 strong. They raised a canvas banner which said: 'Australia Expects Every Man This Day Will Do His Duty' and they elected four leaders to go to the police barracks and say they refused to take out licences. The four leaders were immediately imprisoned and the crowd started to move on the police barracks to rescue them. At this vital moment, a Methodist minister, the Reverend Piddington, jumped on the platform and implored the diggers not to ruin their just cause by shedding of blood. The Reverend Piddington's remarkable powers of oratory swayed the crowd. They lowered their guns, sent another deputation to the police barracks, and their leaders were released and their fines were paid.

The crisis was averted because the diggers were not fundamentally violent revolutionaries. They just wanted to get on with the job without being harassed. But the Goldfields Act failed in its purpose of driving the Turon diggers out to work on the sheep stations. Instead many of them left for the richer fields of Victoria. And there, the flashpoint was still to come.

The Victorian goldfields exploded in 1854 at Ballarat. But it could have happened at Bendigo or Beechworth or a number of other goldfields. The behaviour of the police and the unyielding attitude of the authorities made some kind of collision inevitable. The police seemed to care only for those laws that brought them money. Shanty keepers who paid bribes stayed in business. An American who didn't, Frank Carey, got six months' hard labour for selling two glasses of brandy. Any digger found with a bottle could be charged with grog selling.

A policeman would walk into a man's tent and carry off a bottle of anything worth drinking or not worth drinking that he might find in it and very lucky indeed was the owner if he got off with the mere loss of it. Innumerable instances occurred in which tents were pulled down or burned down, and all their contents destroyed, because small quantities of spirits had been discovered in them.

Even more objectionable was the conduct of the police in the search for licences, the fine sport they used to call digger hunting.

It was a favourite amusement of both officers and men, and it was followed up savagely, relentlessly, and with a refinement of cold blooded cruelty that was not only exasperating, but disgusting in the extreme. Men were chained to trees and logs throughout the blazing heat of day, or the piercing cold of night, whose offences consisted simply in not being able to produce their licences on demand, although they protested, and their statements were often found to be correct, that they had left these precious documents accidentally at home. But unless they had them in their pockets they were placed under arrest.

Governor Charles Joseph Latrobe had become a very unpopular man. When he resigned in 1854 the diggers had high hopes that his successor, Sir Charles Hotham, would abandon the gold licence system. But these hopes were soon disappointed when Hotham decided to increase the licence hunts from once a month to twice a week.

Times were hard on the Eureka fields at Ballarat. The deep alluvial leads had temporarily disappeared and the average digger was making less than labourer's wages. In the words of Rafaello Carboni:

It was a nuggetty Eldorado for the few, a ruinous Field of hard labour for many, a profound ditch of Perdition for Body and Soul to all.

Hotham's redoubled licence hunts enraged the diggers, and the atmosphere became poisonous with hatred of the government and the traps. Diggers chanted in their tents:

Oh the traps, the dirty traps
Kick the traps, whenever you're able
Oh the traps, the dirty traps
Kick the traps right under the table!

The air of the goldfields turned purple with execrations: 'Damn the bloody government, the beaks, the traps, commissioners and all! The robbers! The bushrangers!'

Sir Charles Hotham
Left: *'The License
Inspected', ST Gill*

Sir Charles Hotham was one of history's classic cases of the wrong man in the wrong place at the wrong time. He was fearless, determined and stupid—an ideal choice to head something like the Charge of the Light Brigade. Instead he was sent out to govern Victoria, with instructions from London to balance the colonial budget.

Hotham was not averse to such instructions. He was intensely mean, despite his handsome Governor's salary —£10 000 a year plus £5000 expenses—and made himself a laughing stock when he offered as the only refreshment at the Queen's Birthday Ball a cut-rate beer called 'Murphy's Swipes'. The beer had instantaneous and powerful laxative effects on the 400 guests, who were soon involved in a race to the Government House toilets.

The *Melbourne Morning Herald* referred editorially to 'the storm of indignation, disgust and diarrhoea' produced by 'Mr. Murphy's apparently anti-constipative mixture', and a poet penned an ode to the infamous night:

Police at Eagle Hawk Diggings

When gentlemen made strange wry faces
And walked away with hurrying paces,
And ladies, bending double, strove
To smile and twirl a careless glove
While, secretly they writhed and moan'd
And ere they reached home, fairly groan'd
At having drunk vice-regal swipes
And suffering all these loyal gripes!

Hotham's effect on the diggers was equivalent to the effect of Murphy's Swipes on his guests. He had spent his life in the Royal Navy, and his nickname was 'Old Quarter-deck'. He was a martinet of the old school, one who believed that orders were not to be questioned but simply to be obeyed. He never began to understand the diggers' resentment at being treated like dogs. He should have advised the British Government that the system of gold-fields administration was a disaster. Instead, true to his code, he intensified the system.

It only needed one spark to ignite the situation, and that spark flew at Bentley's Eureka Hotel. James Bentley was an ex-convict. His Eureka Hotel was a favourite haunt of the police, and the Ballarat magistrate D'Ewes had shares in it. On October 7, 1854, two Scots miners, Scobie and Martin, tried to get an after hours drink at the hotel, with fatal results. Mr and Mrs Bentley and a drinking crony, a policeman named Farrell, were annoyed by the hullaballoo of the persistent Scots, and chased them away into the diggings. In the darkness Scobie lost his footing and while he was down he was killed by a blow with a shovel.

The Bentleys and Farrell were brought to trial and were acquitted by the bench of magistrates. The chief magistrate was Bentley's friend and silent partner, D'Ewes.

The Irish diggers at Ballarat were already incensed over the case of Gregorius, the servant of the Catholic priest Father Smyth. Gregorius had been arrested for not having a digger's licence and then convicted of assaulting a trooper. In fact Gregorius didn't have to hold a licence, as a priest's servant, and he was unlikely to damage troopers. He was a cripple.

The Scots were enraged by the acquittal of Bentley and his associates in the Scobie murder case. On October 17 there was a protest meeting of diggers near Bentley's Eureka Hotel, and feelings got out of hand. Defying the presence of the troopers, who rode about in intimidatory fashion, the diggers put the hotel to the torch.

Robert Rede

The *Ballarat Times* blamed the police, and their injudicious show of strength, for the burning of the Eureka Hotel:

> The people are not to be terrified like children, especially men who have stood the working of a Canadian or Gravel Pits sluicer. Such men scorn danger in any form. They have seen the earth, when at the depth of a hundred and fifty feet below the surface, move and tumble in; they have stood the risk of being buried alive underneath, and will such men tremble at the sight of a cap trimmed with silver or gold lace? ... We would advise the Authorities to be careful in their treatment of the miner, the most important class in the country, or they will soon have more on their hands than they in the least suspect.

In the same edition of the *Ballarat Times*, one of the diggers' leaders, J B Humffray, wrote that their grievances went far beyond the Scobie murder case:

> The time has arrived when the people must have the full measure of administrative justice: and if they cannot obtain it according to law they seem determined to take it without law. Justice they have a right to, and must and will have it ... Let the Government

Bentley's Hotel the morning after the fire

take a hint, and anticipate the people's wishes and not wait for their demands and perhaps commands. The land question, the licence question, and the representative question are all questions of moment and must be satisfactorily answered.

As for Bentley's Eureka Hotel, Humffray wrote, it was now:

> . . . a heap of charcoal—its rafters a bundle of crayons with which to write the black history of crime and colonial misrule.

Governor Hotham and his Resident Commissioner at Ballarat, Robert Rede, were not the men who would listen to talk about 'colonial misrule'. They were men who were very impressed by their own uniforms. They stood on their dignity and they stood by their system. To give ground would be to encourage a democratic revolution. The diggers must be taught a fearful lesson, said Hotham and Rede. Troop reinforcements were sent to Ballarat. Three diggers, Fletcher, McIntyre and Westerby, were arrested for the burning of Bentley's Hotel.

DOWN WITH THE LICENSE FEE

DOWN WITH DESPOTISM

"WHO SO BASE AS BE A SLAVE?"

ON

WEDNESDAY NEXT

The 20th Instant, at Two o'clock,

A MEETING

Of all the DIGGERS, STOREKEEPERS, and Inhabitants of Ballarat generally, will be held

ON BAKERY HILL

For the immediate Abolition of the License Fee, and the speedy attainment of the other objects of the Ballarat Reform League. The report of the Dep which have gone to the Lieutenant-Governor to demand the release of the prisoners lately convicted, and to Creswick and forest Creeks, Bendigo, also be submitted at the same time

All who claim the right to a voice in the framing of the Laws under which they should live, are solemnly bound to attend the Meeting further its objects to the utmost extent of their power.

N.B. Bring your Licenses, they may be wanted.

In fact, Hotham and Rede were provoking the thing they most feared. When the diggers failed to win any concessions, they broadened their demands, as Humffray had foreshadowed. The Ballarat Reform League was formed in November 1854 and their mass meetings were no longer talking just about ending the licence system and the police corruption. They were now demanding their own representatives in Parliament, the right for all adult males to vote, a new mining administration and the unlocking of the lands held by the squatters. They sent a deputation, Black, Humffray and Kennedy, to Hotham to demand the release of the three imprisoned diggers. But Sir Charles did not like the word 'demand', and he sent the members of the deputation packing.

The *Ballarat Times,* widely respected by the diggers, was by now denouncing the Government as a tyranny and predicting revolution. The editor, Henry Seekamp, wrote:

'Down with the License Fee'

It is not fines, imprisonment, taxation and bayonets
that is required to keep a people tranquil and content.
It is an attention to their wants and their just rights,
either given to them soon with a good will, or taken
by them later with no will but their own.

In Ballarat in the last week of November 1854, the atmosphere was electric. Hotham had already sent yet another
batch of soldiers to the Ballarat Police Camp. He was
expecting trouble and probably hoping for it. The former
British Navy Commodore wanted a chance to administer
some discipline to the rabble.

On the diggers' side, the moderates were losing ground.
One of the diggers said:

Moral persuasion is all humbug
Nothing convinces like a lick in the lug.

That point seemed to be reinforced when Black, Humffray
and Kennedy had to report back to a giant meeting of diggers that Hotham refused their demand to free the prisoners. Two very important things then happened at that
meeting on Bakery Hill. The diggers voted to burn their
licences and resist arrest, and they raised a new flag.

The *Ballarat Times*, in its report of the monster meeting
of 15 000 diggers on November 29, said:

During the whole of the morning several men were
busily employed in erecting a stage and planting a
flagstaff. This is a splendid pole of about 81 feet and
straight as an arrow. This work being completed
about 11 o'clock, the Southern Cross was hoisted, and
its maiden appearance was a fascinating object to behold. There is no flag in Europe, or in the civilised
world, half so beautiful and Bakery Hill, as being the
first place where the Australian ensign was first
hoisted, will be recorded in the deathless and indelible pages of history. The flag is silk, blue ground with
a large silver cross; no device or arms but all exceed-
ingly chaste and natural.

Sir Charles Hotham called it 'the Australian flag of independence'. Timothy Hayes asked his fellow diggers, 'Will
you die for it?' The flag was made by diggers' wives for the
Canadian rebel, Captain Ross. It was very large and the
cross was white or buff rather than silver. Perhaps the
most significant thing about the Eureka Flag was what
wasn't on it—the Union Jack. The flag was a total rejection
of Hotham and everything he stood for—his Queen, his

The Battle at Eureka Stockade

laws, his licences, his commissioners and his police.

The flag was flying in full view of the military camp. It was a challenge, like the burning of the licences. It was the last possible moment for the Government to back off. But that was not their style. The next day they launched the biggest licence hunt of all time. Rafaello Carboni recalled:

It was a horrible day plagued by the hot winds. A blast of the hurricane winding through gravel pits whirled towards the Eureka this shouting of Joe! By this time a regiment of troopers in full gallop had besieged the whole Eureka, and the traps under their protection ventured amongst the holes. An attempt to give an idea of such disgusting and contemptible campaigns for the search of licences is really odious to an honest man. Are diggers dogs or savages, that they are to be hunted on the diggings, commanded to come out of their holes, and summoned from their tents by these hounds of the executive? . . . Anyone who in Old England went fox hunting can understand pretty well the detestable sport we had then on the gold fields of Victoria.

The Eureka Stockade reconstructed at Ballarat

The police, supported by the military reinforcements from Melbourne, harried the diggers across the Gravel Pits until a group made a stand at Main Road and pelted the troopers with stones. Commissioner Rede read the Riot Act, took prisoners, and ordered a volley fired over the heads of the crowd.

That last licence hunt settled the issue for the diggers. No more was heard from the moderates and the movement was taken over by men who were ready to fight. An armed crowd converged on Bakery Hill. The Irish digger Peter Lalor took over the leadership, and had them swear by the Southern Cross to defend their rights and liberties.

Sir Charles Hotham fully recognised the significance of this event. He wrote:

The Australian flag of independence was solemnly consecrated and vows proffered for its defence . . . A riot was rapidly growing into a revolution.

But it was beyond Hotham to see it as a revolution of decent men against rotten laws. Instead he bayed of 'professional agitators and promoters of sedition . . . foreign

75

democratic opinions . . . overthrow of property and general havoc'.

Peter Lalor later said quite simply why he had come forward to lead the diggers:

> I looked around me; I saw brave and honest men, who had come thousands of miles to labour for independence. I knew that hundreds were in great poverty, who would possess wealth and happiness if allowed to cultivate the wilderness which surrounded us. The grievances under which we had long suffered, and the brutal attack of that day, flashed across my mind; and, with the burning feeling of an injured man, I mounted the stump and proclaimed 'Liberty'.

Peter Lalor called on the armed diggers to form in divisions around the flagstaff and swear allegiance to the Southern Cross. He knelt with his right arm towards the flag and said:

> We swear by the Southern Cross to stand truly by each other, and fight to defend our rights and liberties.

Whereupon, according to Carboni:

> . . . an universal well rounded AMEN was the determined reply, some five hundred right hands stretched towards the flag.

The five hundred sworn rebels, and another thousand supporters, marched behind the Southern Cross to the area called Eureka. There they built a rough stockade of timber slabs, enclosing about an acre of ground. Perhaps it was a place to drill, or a place to shelter from the licence hunts, but nobody was too sure. The diggers had revolutionary sentiments, but they had no General Washington, and no chance to develop any discipline or chain of command.

A council of leaders appointed Peter Lalor as their Commander-in-Chief, but their organisation of forces did not get much beyond that point. Their arms were poor, their military experience practically nil, and they were sitting ducks in the stockade. All they had was courage and the naive conviction that Her Majesty's forces would not attack them on the Sabbath morn. So on Saturday night most of the diggers went home to their tents.

Commissioner Rede's paid informers tipped him off, and on Sunday December 3, 1854, by the dawn's early light, a heavily armed force, more than twice the strength of the diggers, attacked the Eureka Stockade. Taken by surprise, the diggers were quickly overwhelmed. Captain Ross fell mortally wounded. Peter Lalor, his left arm shattered by bullets, was hidden under a heap of timber and later smuggled out of the stockade, swearing, according to a ballad written about the occasion:

You can murder us all in black tyranny's name
But you can't kill the Cross of the South.

A correspondent to the *Geelong Advertiser* reported a piteous scene of slaughtered diggers on the late field of battle:

They all lay in small space with their faces upwards, looking like lead; several of them were still heaving, and at every rise of their breasts, the blood spouted out of their wounds or just bubbled out and trickled away. One man, a stout-chested fine fellow, lay with a pike beside him, he had three contusions in the head, three strokes across the brow, a bayonet wound in the throat under the ear, other wounds on the body—I counted fifteen wounds in that single carcase. Some were bringing handkerchiefs, others had furniture and matting to cover up the faces of the dead. God! sir, it was a sight for a Sabbath morn that, I humbly implore Heaven, may never be seen again. Poor women crying for husbands, and children frightened into quietness ... my soul revolted at such means being so cruelly used by a Government to sustain the law.

The Battle of the Eureka Stockade is not a big entry in the military history books. It was hopelessly one-sided, and it was all over in half an hour. The attackers lost five dead, and the diggers lost thirty. The soldiers trampled the Southern Cross flag, repeatedly bayoneted the wounded and the dead, set fire to tents, attacked innocent bystanders and mistreated over 100 prisoners.

It was a pretty grubby victory, helped along by paid informers and launched on a digger camp that was outnumbered, outgunned and mostly asleep. But it *was* a military victory for His Excellency, Sir Charles Hotham. It was *not* a political victory. Rewards were posted for the capture of the diggers' escaped leaders Frederick Vern, George Black and Peter Lalor, for making war against the Queen. The rewards were spurned by the people of the goldfields.

Most of Melbourne was appalled by the bloodshed at Eureka, and when Hotham insisted on charging thirteen

of the diggers with high treason, no jury would convict
them. As each man was acquitted he was carried shoulder
high from the courtroom by the cheering crowds.

A Royal Commission into the goldfields administration
found the system was rotten and the miners' complaints
fully justified. These were the results:

● The Gold Commissioners were abolished.

● Half the police force was sacked.

● The gold licence tax was abolished and replaced by
an export tax on gold and a miner's right for £1 a year.
The diggers also got the right to elect their own local courts
to regulate mining and to elect their own members of Parliament. Peter Lalor was one of the first men elected.

Just about every demand that Hotham had refused the
moderates, the men of peace, was won at Eureka. Not by
a victory but by a blood sacrifice of diggers. Hotham had
imagined that most of the Stockade rebels were professional agitators and foreign democrats—Americans,
Germans and the like. He also thought they did not rep-
resent the majority of diggers. He was wrong on both
counts. The majority of the Eureka rebels were working
miners and British subjects—men like Happy Jim
Esmond, the discoverer of payable gold in Victoria. And
while a lot of other diggers were against these men taking
up arms, they agreed with their complaints.

And then the way the diggers were overwhelmed, the
sight of their shattered bodies, the shameful behaviour of
the soldiers—all this turned the stomachs of the Victorian
people against Hotham and the system he represented. At
the moment he won this battle, he lost the war. Hotham
himself died one year afterwards, unrepentant and
unloved.

Ballarat has always remembered the Eureka Stockade,
although the memory has been complicated by the passage of a century and a quarter. The rough tracks, the
primitive structures of wood and canvas, the paddocks
that were pitted with miners' shafts like rabbit holes—these
are now the streets and the buildings and the suburbs of
a great provincial city. Many of the actual sites where history was made—the police camp, Bentley's Eureka Hotel—
have been obliterated. But the city abounds with re-
minders of the rebellion.

As if to prove that the Eureka men were not just mad

*Peter Lalor's statue,
Ballarat*

The Eureka Monument, Ballarat

firebrands, Peter Lalor became a rather conservative member of Parliament, and eventually the Speaker. A statue in Sturt Street represents him in his Speaker's wig and gown.

A reconstruction of the Eureka Stockade was opened at Ballarat on the anniversary of the battle, December 3, 1981. Descendants of the people who took part in that struggle were present—not least, Peter Lalor, great-grandson of the diggers' leader. By one of the ironies of history, he's Constable Peter Lalor, of the Victorian Police Force.

There is some local argument as to whether the stockade has been rebuilt in exactly the right place. But for most people the important thing is that it has been rebuilt, in recognition of Ballarat's most momentous day.

The Eureka Stockade was a highly significant event in Australian history. It drew comment from a surprising range of people, not all of them Australian.

Karl Marx: A clash developed, several people were killed, and the gold diggers raised the banner of independence . . . It is not hard to understand that the

79

labouring population rebels against the excessive taxation.

Mark Twain: I think it may be called the finest thing in Australian history. It was a revolution—small in size but great politically; it was a strike for liberty, a struggle for a principle, a stand against injustice and oppression. It is another instance of a victory won by a lost battle. It adds an honourable page to history, the people know it and are proud of it.

Henry Lawson: Twenty minutes freed Australia
                        At Eureka long ago.

Ben Chifley: Eureka was more than an incident or passing phase. It was the first real affirmation of our determination to be the masters of our own political destiny.

Sir Robert Menzies: The Eureka revolution was an earnest attempt at democratic government. It was a fierce desire to achieve true Parliamentary government and true popular control of public finance.

We can't say that Australia had no freedoms before Eureka, and had perfect democracy after it. Our history is much more complicated than that. The struggle for the rights of common people was underway before Eureka, and it was not ended by that battle at the Stockade. But it is plain that the battle was not just a local skirmish at Ballarat over some issue called a gold licence which is now long dead.

When the diggers raised their republican flag, they raised a challenge which still faces Australia—the challenge to assert a completely independent identity, free of the trappings of history, free of any allegiance except to this land alone, the land of the Southern Cross. And by their actions, the diggers asserted a right which we must all hope will *never* need to be exercised again in Australia—the right of free people in a free land to resist tyrannous government, even to death.

Life on the Goldfields

Life on the Australian goldfields was often harsh, sometimes thrilling, seldom dull. The first decade of Australian gold gave rise to some extraordinary episodes, never witnessed before or since in Australian history.

Beechworth's most extravagant moment in the fabulous 1850s, when Victoria was producing forty per cent of the world's gold, is commemorated in the town's Golden Horseshoe monument. It was election day in 1855—the first election since the diggers got the right to vote after the Eureka Stockade battle. There were two factions on the Ovens goldfield—the Punchers who worked the dry banks and gullies and the Monkeys who worked the streams.

The Monkeys marched into town in a huge procession. They sported Napoleon boots and black trousers and they carried banners embellished with solid gold. At their head was their candidate, Daniel Cameron, on a horse shod with golden shoes. The procession came to the Star Hotel, where the two candidates, Cameron and Lyons, presented themselves on the balcony. The diggers in the street voted publicly by a show of miner's rights, and Cameron was the winner.

You could say the streets of Beechworth were paved with gold, because those golden horsehoes lost several ounces weight during the ride through town. But the man who supplied the gold didn't mind. He was Big Johnson, the leader of the Monkeys. When Cameron won the election, Big Johnson shouted three hundred pounds' worth of champagne—enough to make all the people of Beechworth quite happy.

And indeed they had plenty to celebrate. It was more

Golden Horseshoes Monument, Beechworth
Right: *Star Hotel, Beechworth*
Top left: *Re-enactment of Golden Horseshoes procession, Beechworth*
Bottom left: *Re-enactment of the first election at Beechworth*

than the excitement of new political rights and the first democratic election. It was the excitement of living in Victoria's goldfields, which now outshone California's as the richest in the world. The Ovens River district in the northeast of Victoria produced massive quantities of gold from fields like the Woolshed, Pennyweight Flat, Madman's Gully, Sebastopol and Eldorado. Some lucky diggers at the Woolshed sank shafts straight into gold deposits which made them rich men in a day.

Beechworth was the capital of the Ovens goldfield, and the gold came into the Beechworth banks before it was carried by the escorts to Melbourne. The bank records tell an amazing story of gold production. In the ten years from 1852 over four million ounces or 153 tons of gold were sent away from Beechworth. Taking an average 1980s figure for gold of $400 an ounce, it was worth $3649 million. And that was not from all Victoria. That was just from the one town, Beechworth.

The prosperity showed. Within those ten years, Beechworth was transformed from a patch of bush called May Day Hills into the most important town on the old Sydney-Melbourne highway, headquarters of a district of forty thousand people. Gold was the main business of the town. In their magazine the miners stored the gunpowder which they used to blast the gold out of 'them thar hills'. The gold was taken away regularly to Melbourne under heavily armed escorts from the Gold Office and Sub-Treasury.

The troopers who occupied the police building were not the only armed men about. Most of the early diggers on the Ovens carried guns and some were quick to use them. There were fifteen murders in the first six months of the goldfield and business was brisk at the Courthouse. Bushrangers preyed on the gold escorts and the gold diggers, and a bushranger named Sheehan was the first man hanged at Beechworth Gaol, many years before the Kellys were cooped up behind its massive walls.

Bushranging was to become big business in the days of gold, and there were plenty of wild colonial boys who preferred to take short cuts to fortune. In 1852 bushrangers staged an audacious holdup on the St Kilda Road, Melbourne. The artist William Strutt painted this scene, in which the immigrants are obviously wondering what manner of country they have come to, while the bushrangers already look like a race apart.

The gold escort with its rich cargo posed an irresistible challenge to the bushrangers. There were many attacks on the escorts. The most notorious was staged by Frank Gardiner's gang at Eugowra Rocks in 1862. Fourteen thousand pounds' worth of gold from Forbes goldfield was captured en route to Orange, and much of it was never recovered. It was the nineteenth century's version of the Great Train Robbery and it gave rise to the most mettlesome of bushranger ballads:

> *It's all about bold Frank Gardiner*
> *With the devil in his eye*
> *He said: 'We've work before us, boys*
> *We've got to do or die*
> *So blacken up your faces*
> *Before the fall of night*
> *And over by Eugowra Rocks*
> *We'll either fall or fight.*

> *We'll stop the Orange escort*
> *With powder and with ball*
> *We'll shoot the coach to pieces*
> *And we'll down the peelers all*
> *And we'll lift the diggers' money*
> *And collar all their gold*
> *So mind your guns are killers now*
> *My comrades true and bold.'*

'Bailing Up the Royal Mail',
ST Gill

So now off go the rifles
The battle has begun
The escort started running, lads
Before the setting sun
The outlaws seized their plunder
So saucy and so bold
They're riding from Eugowra Rocks
Encumbered with the gold.

And as with savage laughter
They left the fatal place
They cried, 'We've struck bonanza, boys
We've won the steeplechase.'
And Gardiner their leader
He shouted loud 'Hooray!
I think we've made our fortunes
At Eugowra Rocks today.'

You can sing of Johnny Gilbert
Dan Morgan and Ben Hall
But the brave and reckless Gardiner
He's the boy to beat them all.

'Bushrangers on the St Kilda Road,' William Strutt (detail)

It was a violent time. Men bore arms to protect their gold, or to rob other people's gold, and an amazing array of guns and other weapons could be seen on the goldfields. They varied from shotguns, carbines and blunderbusses to cheap Belgian pistols and tiny Derringers carried by ladies

'Bushrangers on the St Kilda Road', William Strutt (detail)

for their protection on coach journeys. However, the standard weapons were the Bowie knife, sometimes called the 'Diggers Friend', and the Colt revolver. It was the habit of the diggers to fire off their Colts around sundown each night to ensure they were in working order and to warn off thieves who might be thinking of slitting a hole in their tent and stealing their gold during the night.

The goldfields were no place for people who suffered from insomnia or tender ears. As one digger described it:

The hillsides were lined with tents, and towards sundown the forest resounded with the blows of a thousand axes. The scene at night, when the large wood fires were blazing in front of every tent, was peculiarly weird, and somewhat resembled a huge military encampment. The woods echoed with constant explosions of firearms as the diggers let off their revolvers preparatory to re-loading for the night—a needful precaution against the possible attempts of the lawless members of society who frequented every

rush. The uproar continued, with ceaseless shouting, far into the night, until, wearied out, all at length retired to rest.

'The Sickly Digger', ST Gill

Most of the deaths in early Beechworth were not from violent causes, but from ailments like typhoid which were common on the goldfields and which left the old Ovens District hospital filled to capacity. Medical knowledge was in short supply and so was book learning of any kind. But the citizens did their best to improve themselves and they subscribed money to build a lecture hall and reading room, supplied with all current newspapers and periodicals. This became the Public Library and Burke Museum, named for the explorer Robert O'Hara Burke who was once superintendent of police at Beechworth. A local legend claims that Burke was an absent-minded chap who once got lost between the main street and his own house— hardly a promising sign for his future explorations. But the legend may not be true. In any case, Burke was well liked in a town where the police were not always looked upon fondly by a turbulent population.

Goldfield undertaker

Beechworth had sixty hotels and saloons in its roaring days. They ranged from crude shanties to substantial brick buildings with the plushest of fittings. Some had gambling tables with special recesses where you parked your gold sovereigns. A man could lose his money in elegant surroundings. What was a trifling loss to a race of men who fired gold out of shotguns and sprinkled it on Christmas puddings and played skittles with full champagne bottles and fed buttered pound notes to their favourite dogs? An old-timer recalled:

89

Left: *A gambling table in Tanswells' Commercial Hotel, Beechworth*
Top right: *Tanswells' Commercial Hotel, Beechworth*
Bottom right: *United States Hotel, Sovereign Hill, Ballarat*

The pastime of the lucky digger often consisted of a reckless indulgence in champagne and furious driving. Some diggers amused themselves by loading their guns with nuggets of gold as a substitute for leaden bullets, and firing at gumtrees. I was one of a party who partook of a golden plum pudding, prepared for our Christmas dinner in 1853. About half an ounce of fine gold was washed out from the gravelly bed of Forest Creek and mixed with the other ingredients of the pudding—so easy was it to procure the precious metal.

The heady excitement of those days of gold, when it seemed that fortunes were there for the taking, was celebrated in a well-known folk song:

When first I left old England's shore
Such yarns as we were told
As how folks in Australia
Could pick up lumps of gold
So when we got to Melbourne Town
We were ready soon to slip
And get even with the captain
All hands scuttled from the ship.

We steered our course for Geelong Town
Then north-west to Ballarat
Where some of us got mighty thin
And some got sleek and fat
Some tried their luck at Bendigo
And some at Fury Creek
I made a fortune in a day
And spent it in a week.

With my swag all on my shoulder
Black billy in my hand
I travelled the bush of Australia
Like a true-born native man.

J F Hughes, the miner who shared in the golden Christmas pudding, reported that true-born native men, and every other kind of man, could be met on the goldfields:

Porcupines Flat had now rapidly developed into a gigantic rush of some 40 000 people. Among those busy gold seekers might have been found representatives of nearly every phase of human society—from the Aboriginal, the ticket-of-leave men from the Derwent, the stockman from Riverina to the enterprising merchant and the Oxford graduate. A long row of canvas tents and calico stores, with their distinguishing flags, were quickly run up, forming a busy and exciting scene, enlivened by the ceaseless winding of windlasses and rocking of cradles along the lead, and now and again might be heard above the din the voice of some newsvendor calling out: 'Latest English news!' about the Russian war and the bombardment of Sebastopol.

Several restaurants and music halls were erected; at one of the latter flourished a prominent character in the person of the satirist Thatcher—vulgarly pronounced 'Thrasher'—generally known as the diggers' poet, who appeared in a manner born for the times.

He accurately caricatured the habits of the people, and satirised the pompous demeanour of the gold-laced officials with effect; and, in his rough and unmetrical verse, recorded a strong protest against the treatment of the diggers by the dominant faction.

An excellent specimen of his style may be found in that satirical stanza, commencing:

> *On the fields of Ballarat*
> *You're scarce allowed to wear your hat!*

His entertainments attracted large crowds, and he delighted his audiences with comic parodies upon favourite songs set to favourite airs.

Thatcher's popularity amongst the diggers rested on more than his ability to lampoon their enemies. He had the knack of capturing and putting into song the diggers' atti-

tudes towards themselves, their pride in their labour, and
their unfailing zest for a good time:

*United States Hotel and
Victoria Theatre, Sovereign
Hill, Ballarat*

> *When we're out upon the spree*
> *Oh, what jolly dogs are we*
> *We spend our tin and shout for young and old*
> *The liquor we enjoy*
> *Our mirth has no alloy*
> *And merrily we flash about our gold*
> *We drink to all the gals*
> *And seated with all our pals*
> *We enjoy ourselves like Britons, free from care*
> *And we make the whole place ring*
> *With our voices as we sing*
> *Oh jolly is the digger when the gold's all there.*

There is no doubt that the diggers liked to be jolly dogs
and to flash about their gold while they had it, which often
was not very long. One of their favourite carousing spots
was the Victoria Theatre in Ballarat, now open again as

part of Ballarat's superb re-creation of the gold era, at Sovereign Hill. A fair example of the rip-roaring spirit of the goldfields was that theatre's opening night in 1856.

The star turn of the evening was Lola Montez, a lady with many dubious pasts. Her real name was Maria Dolores Eliza Rosanna Gilbert and she was born in 1818 in Limerick, Ireland. But her first appearance on the London stage was as 'Lola Montez, a Spanish dancer'. Lola's major talents emerged in the dressing room rather than on the stage. On a tour of Europe, she acquired and shed three husbands and a long string of lovers. They included Emperor Ludwig of Bavaria, and, after that affair, Lola styled herself Countess of Landsfeld.

Tiring of Europe, Lola set out to conquer California, and was greeted on arrival as 'The very *Comet* of her sex'. The critics changed their opinion after seeing her stage act, in which she postured about raining fake spiders from her skirts, and she retired 'shorn of glory' as one critic put it, and 'trailing clouds of wickedness'.

The so-called smouldering sensuality of her Spider Dance had been laughed off the stage in San Francisco, but it tickled the fancy of the Ballarat diggers when she arrived there fresh, more or less, from California. However, the applause was not universal. Henry Seekamp, the editor of the *Ballarat Times*, denounced 'the unhealthy excitement fostered by one whose notoriety is of an unenviable kind'.

Henry Seekamp was a fiery little man. He'd already served three months in prison because of his pro-digger editorials at the time of the Eureka Stockade, which were judged to be seditious. Now he had stirred an unhealthy excitement in Lola Montez, and she announced her intention of horsewhipping 'the great gentleman who attacks poor little innocent me'.

Sure enough, Lola Montez descended on Seekamp like an avenging fury at the United States Hotel. But Henry had been warned of the lady's intentions, and he too was packing a whip. When she laid about him, he responded with equal vigour. There was a battle of Trojan proportions, with much hair-pulling and shouting of insults, and eventually Seekamp decamped from the field of battle leaving Montez with whip rampant. But the final honours were pretty even. *Melbourne Punch* summed up:

> *Erle Seekamp's face bore bloody trace*
> *Of Lola Montez's lash*
> *Her shoulders fair, if they were bare,*
> *Would show a crimson gash.*

The fiery spirits which surfaced on the occasions like these were not unconnected with the fiery spirits served at the bars of Ballarat, in concoctions like brandy smash, sherry cobbler, whisky milk punch and redoubtable specials like the Ballarat Knocker, a high octane mixture of Jamaica rum, cayenne pepper, opium and metho.

Australia had no iceworks before the 1860s and the drinks in bars were cooled by ice imported all the way from America. It was cut from ponds in Massachusetts, stored in ice houses in Boston, packed in sawdust in the hulls of sailing ships bound for Australia, and then hauled

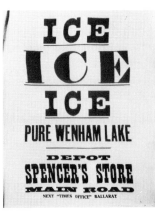

Ice Poster

from Melbourne to the goldfields on bullock drays. It seems incredible now. In those days it was offered as an excuse for the incredible price of the drinks. Any ice left in a glass was tipped into fresh drinks. After a few Ballarat Knockers, the diggers were in the right frame of mind to roll into the Theatre and hear their favourite bard, Charles Thatcher, describe the capers of the rowdies who ruled the Ballarat streets:

This Ballarat's a curious spot
At least I'm sure I've found it so
Bad luck is sure to be my lot
No matter to what part I go
I really do feel quite unnerved
In fact it nearly makes me sob
To think how shamefully I'm served
By that disgraceful rowdy mob.

If to the theatre I go
Or to the Charlie for a dance
A fight begins and then I know
I don't stand even half a chance
Although I try to walk away
I'm sure to get one for my nob
'That's him' some cove is sure to say
So I'm mauled by the rowdy mob.

I've freely spoken out my mind
To do so is my sole relief
This song though doleful is, I find
My only safety valve for grief
Although some cove may knock me flat
For saying this, so help me bob
I'm confident that Ballarat
Is governed by the rowdy mob.

Thatcher was only half joking in that song. He was well built and knew how to defend himself. It was just as well, since he was attacked a couple of times by citizens who didn't relish being featured in his satirical songs

Everyone on the goldfields had their own particular crosses to bear. Some were revealed in the rough notices which were pinned on trees, tents and post office walls:

Pat Flynn calls on Biddy to return to the tint forninst the crossroads.

The laundress who took away the clothes from the *Times* office, about a week since, is requested to return the said clothes, washed or unwashed, without delay.

James Dakin notyces the publik agin trustin his wife.

If the person who kindly borrowed my Meerschaum Pipe, on Thursday evening, will come to the United States Hotel Bar, I will give him Pipe Case and Tobacco, those articles being of no value to me now.

My wife Elizabeth Blenkinson having gone away with Jim the Sawyer I will not be responsible for your debts and have nothing more to say to you.

Ten Pounds Reward for my Black Mare.
No questions asked nor ideas insinuated.

By the middle of the 1850s, life for women on the goldfields was still fairly primitive, but at least Ballarat had advanced from the earliest days of tents and humpies and hardly any women at all. By the late 1850s, miners' families were occupying weatherboard cottages with perhaps a patch of garden. And inside, a woman's touch might be seen in the furnishing of mats and cushions and curtains and kitchenware.

Stores now carried a wide variety of wares. This advertisement for a Buninyong store was penned in the 1850s by Robert Boyle, great-great-grandfather of the Olympic runner, Raelene Boyle:

> Ye diggers who have found the gold
> And want to spend your money
> Come listen to the tale here told
> You'll find it very funny.
>
> Come to our store for what you need
> We have it, never doubt it
> It must be very scarce indeed
> If we should be without it.

Top right: *Waterloo Store, Sovereign Hill, Ballarat*
Bottom right: *The Ballarat Times and Clarke the Grocer, Sovereign Hill, Ballarat*

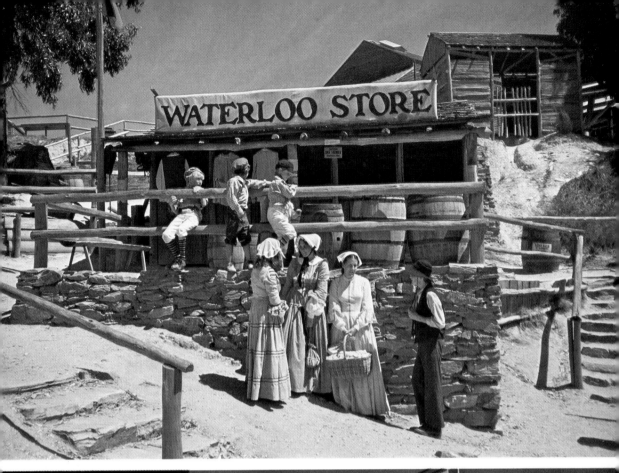

A list of what we have to sell
Is here to you presented
Come to our store, we'll use you well
And you shall be contented.

We've almonds, figs and muscatels
We've axes and pickhandles
We've carters' whips and bullock bells
And boots and tallow candles.

We've wafers, pens and ink and nails
And various kinds of papers
Quart pots and pannikins and pails
And castor oil and capers.

We've fishing hooks and fishing lines
Yes and we have some fishes
(Herrings I mean) We've ropes and twines
Zinc buckets and tin dishes

And would you think? We have eggs
Though some perhaps are addle
We've lines for clothes and eke clothes pegs
A bridle and a saddle.

We've blankets, rings and frying pans
We've hammers, saws and nippers
And cups and colanders and cans
And puddling tubs and dippers.

We've curry powder, mustard too
Which may your palate tickle
We've soap and soda, starch and blue
And every kind of pickle.

Cigars and snuff and bottled fruits
(We do not give them gratis)
And then we've those delicious roots
Which Irishmen call 'Praties'.

Ask us for anything you please
You'll find there's nothing lacking
Tobacco, matches, English cheese
And pickled pork and blacking.

But brandy's what we do not sell
It might cause some vexation
If anyone should go and tell
For then comes confiscation.

'John Aloo's Dining
Rooms, Ballarat', ST Gill

So if you're thirsty take a drink
Which won't hurt anybody
This, many sober people think,
Better than grog or toddy.

What'er you want we have it here
You cannot be mistaken
We've lemonade and ginger beer
Superior hams and bacons.

Regatta shirts – shirts of Scotch twill
Blue shirts and shooting jackets
Hair and tooth brushes if you will
And envelopes in packets.

Alpaca coats and cotton socks
Jumpers in colour shining
Muslin de laine for ladies' frocks
And calico for lining.

And we can for a lady find
A beautiful straw bonnet
And also if she is inclined
Ribbon to put upon it.

Gold diggers' guides and magazines
Threads, needles and stay laces
And tea and coffee and sardines
And handkerchiefs and braces.

We've flour and butter, sugar, rice
And candied peel (do take it)
You'll have a pudding in a trice
If you know how to make it.

We've sago, barley, arrowroot
And everything that nice is
Currants and all that kind of fruit
With cinnamon and spices.

Eau de Cologne and pocket knives
Hair oil and black lead pencils
Tea kettles for your thrifty wives
And all kind of utensils.

And now I think it's time to stop
There's more but never mind it
Whate'er you want this is the shop
Where you are sure to find it.

Top right: *Cobb & Co Coach*
Bottom right: *Coach and horses, Sovereign Hill, Ballarat*

Transport had improved since the first days of the gold rushes. The new railways which were just beginning to appear in the cities were still a long way from the goldfields, and goods were slow to arrive, but passengers travelled more briskly in the smart Concord coaches introduced by Freeman Cobb and his American associates.

In this scheme of transport the wheelwright played a key part. He was one of the artisans whose skills were essential to goldfields life. The tinsmith was another. He turned out frying pans, buckets, billies, plates and mugs and lanterns, jugs and containers and hipbaths—many things the miner required at home, plus one indispensable item for the miner at work—the gold pan.

The art of panning, of washing out the dirt and keeping the alluvial gold, was just one of many arts and skills that the early diggers needed to survive on the goldfields. Many

things were hard to get and expensive to buy, for instance cradles, which accelerated the process of washing off dirt and gravel while trapping the gold. Diggers thought nothing of knocking together their own cradles from a few bits of wood and an old blanket.

Sometimes they built an extended gold-trapping box called a Long Tom. And if they had no water to wash the dirt through the Long Tom, they brought the water from a creek by building a flume, a sort of wooden pipeline.

Probably the best example of the craft of those early diggers is the windlass, the basic machine for bringing buckets of dirt up from the shaft. These machines were not mass-produced by factories, they could not be ordered in by train from Melbourne. The diggers had to improvise, and they did it cleverly, using the timber closest at hand, making their joins without nails, and producing machines that worked efficiently.

It was said that the alluvial gold digger of the 1850s needed to be a jack-of-all-trades and master of most. Many of these practical men arrived at the practical conclusion that there were better ways of making gold than digging it. And the same skills that built windlasses were turned to building furniture for the captive local market— everything from four poster beds to spinning wheels.

The sailmaker's trade, like the sailors themselves, transferred with ease from the sailing ships to the goldfields. Canvas goods of all kinds were indispensable, from the humble waterbag to the storekeeper's flags. The product most in demand was the tent—a reminder that many of the alluvial diggers had the same roving gipsy life as sailors. Some ideas from the old sailing ships proved useful in the goldfields. For instance, the windsail, used to ventilate ships below decks, was adapted to catch fresh air and force it down the mining shafts.

The king of all the goldfields tradesmen was the blacksmith. The clang of his hammer was heard wherever diggers worked. His forge produced a great variety of items which they needed and for which they had to pay handsomely. It was remarked that the blacksmiths managed to hammer a good many ounces out of the diggers. Two shillings to sharpen a pick, six shillings to lay on a new piece of steel.

Shoeing horses was a regular part of the blacksmith's work. And other goldfields businessmen also made a

Whim and diggers

handsome living out of the horse. Saddlers provided their gear and harness. Livery stables provided board and lodging for the most important animals on the goldfields. Horses were central to the alluvial digger's way of life. They provided his individual means of transport and they pulled his passenger coaches.

They were also quickly harnessed to relieve men of some of the more backbreaking work of gold mining. By a simple device called a whip, which was just a rope slung over a pulley, horses were used to raise the heavy buckets from the shaft. A whim was another device to do the same job. The horse walked around a central drum which simultaneously raised and lowered buckets in twin shafts.

One group of miners used a horse-driven machine to break up stiff clay washdirt and release the gold. These men were called puddlers and they were unpopular be-

cause of all the slush they produced. But they regarded themselves as a special breed of man, and the backbone of the Bendigo field.

Above left: *The Blacksmith*
Above right: *Windlass*

> *They want to stop our puddling, as many of you know*
> *Contractors say that of our slush there is an overflow*
> *But if they stop us they'll be sure to injure Bendigo.*
>
> *If you crush the puddling interest and stay the*
> *   puddler's hand*
> *What becomes of your fine buildings here that on the*
> *   township stand*
> *The commerce of this district then would sink down*
> *   precious low.*
>
> *The winter soon is coming and our dams will then be*
> *   full*
> *We'll run the stuff through the machines and then we'll*
> *   have a pull*
> *And in its pristine glory will shine forth Bendigo.*
> *Drive on, my lads, heigho, wash on my lads heigho*
> *For who can lead the life that we jolly puddlers do.*

Above left: *Gold panning*
Above right: *Puddling*

Despite their confidence, the puddlers were a dying race, although one of them was adaptable enough to make the business keep paying. A Scot named George Guthrie was not getting much gold, but he liked the quality of the clay, and he decided to return to his former trade as a potter. With one boy, a barrow and a kick wheel, he started the Bendigo Pottery in 1857. It became one of the great institutions of the goldfields and produced many fine pieces of work and a world-wide reputation.

The days of the alluvial miners on the great Victorian fields like Ballarat and Bendigo were drawing to a close after those first ten feverish years of the 1850s. They had one machine that pointed the way to the future—the Chilean mill, used to crunch out the gold which was now being found in quartz rock rather than gravel. This simple one horse power machine was soon to be replaced by mechanical quartz crushers.

The alluvial digger was also to be replaced in the next era by hard rock miners drilling deep underground for big companies. But he didn't know that and he liked to immortalise himself in the photographic rooms of the time as the proud, free and independent digger—the Ballarat man.

> There's a place that bears a well known name
> It has a township and a flat
> It's first of all in colonial fame
> And called Old Ballarat

107

There are other goldfields, Castlemaine,
The Ovens, Bendigo
But Ballaratians it's quite plain
They by its side can't show.

It's a thing to be proud of, deny it who can,
It's a thing to be proud of, deny it who can,
It's a thing to be proud of, deny it who can,
If you're able to say I'm a Ballarat man.

Joey Gougenheim

Many of our impressions of early goldfields life come from ST Gill. He was the artist of the era, as Charles Thatcher was the singer of the era. Neither man was as lucky as some of the diggers they celebrated. Thatcher died of cholera in Shanghai. Gill expired as a drink-sodden and unidentified derelict on the steps of the Melbourne Post Office, and was buried in a pauper's grave.

A third man, who was not much luckier in his own life, could be described as the poet of the goldfields. He wrote the lines:

Their shining Eldorado
Beneath the southern skies
Was day and night forever
Before their eager eyes
The brooding bush, awakened,
Was stirred in wild unrest
And all the year a human stream
Went pouring to the West.

Henry Lawson's poem 'The Roaring Days' was based on his bitter-sweet boyhood in Gulgong, New South Wales, which he remembered, he said, as a boy would remember his first and only pantomime.

Oh, who would paint a goldfield
And paint the picture right
As old Adventure saw it
In early morning's light?
The yellow mounds of mullock
With spots of red and white
The scattered quartz that glistened
Like diamonds in light.

The azure line of ridges
The bush of darkest green
The little homes of calico
That dotted all the scene
The flat straw hats, with ribands

Maggie Oliver

That old engravings show
The dress that still reminds us
Of sailors long ago.

I hear the fall of timber
From the distant flats and fells
The peeling of the anvils
As clear as little bells
The rattle of the cradle
The clash of windlass-boles
The flutter of the crimson flags
Above the golden holes.

The Gulgong diggers were nothing if not confident. They called their town the Hub of the World. And history and a growing sense of national consciousness justified their confidence. Gulgong has become the town on the ten dollar note, and there Henry Lawson gazes forever at the scenes of his youth.

No living town in Australia has survived unchanged over a century, and none has been unscathed by the onslaught of the motor car. But Gulgong more than most gold towns retains in its streets and its old buildings a sense, an echo, of the Roaring Days. There are still scenes that would not seem strange to the ghost of Henry Lawson. Henry wrote:

Rough built stages and theatres
Where the world's best actors trod
Singers bringing reckless rovers
Nearer boyhood, home and God—
Paid in laughter, tears and nuggets
In the drama fortune plays—
'Tis the palmy days of Gulgong—
Gulgong in the Roaring Days!

He was referring to Cogden's Assembly Rooms, a theatre opened by John Hart Cogden, who had a troupe with the wonderfully eccentric name of the Iron Clad Minstrels.

The theatre soon took on a grander name, which it still retains—the Prince of Wales Opera House. The *Gulgong Guardian* of Lawson's day did not agree that it was rough built. The local paper reported how keenly the audience appreciated 'so comfortable and commodious a theatre'. That was on the occasion of the appearance of 'the world renowned Miss Joey Gougenheim'. At least, she was world renowned in 1871.

Joey Gougenheim, Charles Young, Maggie Oliver, Mrs Darnell, Lizzie Morgan, are some of the names forgotten now, but celebrated a century ago when they trod the boards at Gulgong. Lawson recorded how the miners snatched the horses out of harness and pulled Maggie Oliver's coach into town, how they showered her with gold nuggets on stage and fought over pieces of her sailor's hat which she threw to them when the coach took her away.

As well as those ancient melodramas where the diggers heartily hissed the villain and cheered the hero to the echo, the Gulgong Opera House was the scene of many famous balls and dances. Waltzing was all the go, and according to local legend, the diggers of the 1870s learned to waltz there with eggshells strapped to their heels, following the commandment that the heels of a good waltzer should never touch the ground. And in the absence of female partners, it was said that they learned to waltz while cradling their swags in their arms—they were literally waltzing

Prince of Wales Opera House, Gulgong

National School,
Sovereign Hill,
Ballarat

Matilda. 'Matilda' was an old German slang word for the digger's swag, and the waltzing customs of the Gulgong diggers may have given birth to the phrase which Banjo Paterson used, twenty years later, in the most famous of all Australian songs.

The civilisation of the early Australian goldfields was pretty much the same the whole country over. Far away from Gulgong in New South Wales, the diggers at Tarnagulla in the western Victorian goldfields cheered the same heroes, hissed the same villains and waltzed to the same tunes in their Victoria Theatre on Saturday night. And on Sunday morning came the reckoning.

They were no longer just harum-scarum gypsies. They were becoming respectable settled men, family men, and a goodly number of families went to church on Sundays. They had a wide choice of churches, though perhaps they had a problem to reconcile what they heard on Sundays with the quest for gold that occupied them through the rest of the week. The preacher might exhort them:

> And I say unto ye brethren, in the very words of the
> Bible, 'Neither shall he greatly multiply to himself sil-
> ver and gold'. 'The silver is mine and the gold is mine,
> saith the Lord of Hosts.' 'Go to now, ye rich men,
> weep and howl for the miseries that shall come upon
> you. Your riches are corrupted and your garments are
> motheaten. Your gold and silver is cankered, and the
> rust of them shall be a witness against you, and shall
> eat your flesh as it were fire. Ye have heaped treasure
> together for the last days.' But I say to you, 'It is easier
> for a camel to go through the eye of a needle than for
> a rich man to enter into the kingdom of God.'

But what was gold digging if not the raw and undisguised
scramble for riches, the dream of heaping up treasure, the
lust for fine gold? And what digger did not pray for the ulti-
mate lucky strike, the discovery of a great nugget of gold
that would make his fortune in an instant? Many found the
lure of gold stronger than the lure of God. In *Australia Felix*
Henry Handel Richardson wrote:

> There were those who, having once seen the metal in
> the raw: in dust, fine as that brushed from a butter-
> fly's wing; in heavy, chubby nuggets; or, more exquis-
> ite still, as the daffodil-yellow veining of bluish-white
> quartz: these were gripped in the subtlest way of all.
> A passion for the gold itself awoke in them an almost
> sensual craving to touch and possess; and the glitter
> of a few specks at the bottom of pan or cradle came
> in time to mean more to them than 'Home' or wife,
> or child.

Victoria was able to incite the 'unholy hunger' for gold
with temptations more compelling than a few specks in a
pan. In 1858 twenty-two Cornishmen working a shaft on
Bakery Hill, Ballarat, hit the biggest nugget of gold ever
recorded in the world to that time. The 'Welcome Nugget'
weighed 2217 ounces and was sold for nearly £9000.

A succession of nuggets was found in Victoria, each bigger than anything found in California or anywhere else.
Out of forty-seven great nuggets recorded in world history,
forty were found in Australia and thirty-two of them in
central Victoria. An area of land between Bendigo, Maryborough and Wedderburn was so rich in nuggets that it became known as the Golden Triangle. And it was at
Moliagul in the Golden Triangle that the daddy of them all,

the biggest nugget that has ever been known, was found in 1869. It was the 'Welcome Stranger'. It was turned up by two prospectors, Deason and Oates, and it weighed 2284 ounces. A monument in Dunolly commemorates the anvil on which that leviathan nugget had to be broken up before it could be weighed at the Dunolly Bank. Left intact, it would in time have been worth a fabulous fortune. But Deason and Oates had no time to spare. They were broke and very glad to take the money for the weight of gold the nugget yielded. For them, at long last, the golden dream had come true.

The early diggers were torn between conflicting loyalties to the dictates of religion and the quest for gold; to the old countries where most of them came from and to the new country where they sought their fortunes. It was their children who became Australians and were to see Australia develop from a collection of colonies into one nation.

The Red Hill National School at Ballarat is a re-creation of the school system of the 1850s on which the later State schools were based. Here visiting schoolchildren can experience the lessons their great-grandparents were taught. And in the playground, the simple games they played in the 1850s, with hoops and tops and horseshoes.

The standards of education of the diggers themselves varied widely. Many had not enjoyed the benefits of much formal schooling. But it was the great age of self-improvement. Mechanics Institutes like the one at Ballarat sprang up across the country. The chess club that began there was the first in Australia. Concerts were given, there were talks and lectures, and from the range of books and the great variety of newspapers and magazines that were brought in from around the world, we can get some idea of the diggers' earnest attempts to advance their own knowledge, and to keep up with what was happening in the world.

It was a European way of life transplanted to Australia, which was hardly surprising. Seventy per cent of the Victorian population in 1861 was born overseas and sixty per cent in the British Isles. But there was one significant element from overseas which did not fit into this pattern. Eight per cent of the Victorian population and one in five of the male population in 1860 was Chinese.

The Chinese temple was a familiar sight on the gold-

fields. At least they called it a temple. The Europeans called it a joss house and suspected it was the home of dark and heathenish practices.

Joss House interior, Bendigo

Suspicion and hatred dogged relations between the white and Chinese diggers and led to outbreaks of violence at Buckland River and other goldfields. The violence came from the whites and there were two main causes. One was the white man's conviction, which was not limited to Australia in the nineteenth century, that coloured races were inferior. The other was the fear of economic competition. The Chinese were tireless and efficient gold seekers and whenever things went badly for the whites, they seized on the Chinese as scapegoats. The most notorious of these incidents occurred at Lambing Flat, New South Wales, in 1861 when two thousand white diggers attacked the Chinese camp.

But the major Chinese settlements of those times were in Victoria. One of the biggest Chinese camps was at Beechworth. Several thousand Chinese settled there after they were driven out of the Buckland Valley by violence from white diggers in 1857. There's little visible evidence now of that Chinese camp, but the relics are still there for those who are prepared to dig, like the gold miners did.

Burning Towers, Chinese Cemetery, Beechworth

The most visible evidence of the Chinese presence at Beechworth can be seen in the cemetery. Hundreds of Chinese were buried there and their graves are marked by headstones. The Chinese Burning Towers were their letter-box to Heaven. Prayers and letters to the gods were placed inside and burnt and so translated into the spirit world. Perhaps some of their communications to the spirits dealt with the hostility of the white man in Australia.

For all the provocation they suffered, only one Chinese digger is known to have reacted by turning bushranger. His name was Sam Poo, and his career as a highwayman on the Mudgee roads was brief and highly unsuccessful, ending with his execution for the shooting of a policeman.

The biggest hazard to the gold digger was not the bushranger's gun, but the conditions of the early goldfields, the hard and exposed life, the poor water supplies and the primitive state of medical science. Doctors' instruments of the day looked more like instruments of medieval torture. The setting of broken bones without anaesthetic came very close to torture, while the doctors' pills and nostrums were quite ineffective against the deadliest killers of the day, pneumonia and typhoid (or 'colonial fever').

Sometimes the doctor's treatment was worse than the disease. There was no law to prevent anyone setting himself up as a doctor on the goldfields and many of them were utter quacks—clerks and drapers' assistants pretending to be surgeons. They operated with the same knives they used to chop up tobacco and spread their butter.

In the case of a Bendigo digger who was shot through the neck in a fight, one quack doctor tried to nourish the man by bandaging pieces of raw steak on his stomach. When this didn't work, he poured wine into him but it all came out of the hole in his neck. Naturally the digger died. And naturally a lot of other diggers avoided doctors altogether. They preferred to treat their own complaints with Holloway's Pills, which contained a powerful charge of opium.

Early death came to many of the first Australian gold diggers and among the monuments they left are the numerous and well-filled graveyards which are scattered through the Australian countryside. The cemetery at Warrandyte, on the upper Yarra River, was the site of one of the first gold rushes in Victoria, and generations of diggers are buried there. Curiously that different sort of digger, the gravedigger, was never in short supply. The graves were dug very carefully, many strangers turned up at funerals and inspected the holes with keen eyes, the earth from the graves was washed by the gravediggers. They believed the lost gold reefs of Warrandyte passed under the cemetery. Such was the grip gold had on people, even to the grave.

The alluvial gold of Victoria and New South Wales petered out in the 1860s. It was the death of that first fantastic lottery of gold for the individual digger, but it had made Australia another country. The land of exile had been changed into the land of promise, and half a million new people had come here. There were new trades and markets, and new towns dotted the inland. Melbourne was now the largest city. The squatters still gripped the broad acres, but political democracy was advancing and Australia stood on the brink of a golden age of prosperity—a golden age built on the gold of the Australian earth.

The Golden Age

The hey-day of the free and independent digger soon passed from Australian history like a golden dream. Within ten years of the first Australian gold rushes of 1851, the sight and sound of big machinery ushered in a new era of gold mining. It was to be a Golden Age in Australian civilisation, though not for the individual digger. Now it was the day of the promoters, the investors and the company men—men who could raise the capital to buy and operate the machinery.

The major Victorian fields like Ballarat and Bendigo had for ten years produced nearly half the world's output of gold. But now their alluvial gold was reaching exhaustion. The remaining treasure was locked in quartz rock. It had to be recovered from deep underground, brought to the surface and pounded out of the rock by great machines. The stamper battery replaced the windlass as the symbol of this new age.

Up in the wild mountains of Gippsland, the sounds of the Mountaineers' Brass Band competed with the endless turmoil of the stampers in the Long Tunnel Battery at Walhalla. This was a town besieged by bitter weather, flood, fire and isolation in the remote ranges. It was so steep that everything in the town travelled upwards. The miners walked up the hill to the mines, even higher up the hill to the church on Sunday, and when they died they were taken higher than heaven itself to the cemetery on top of the ridge above Walhalla.

The town had not only brass bands and churches, but numerous shops and hotels, a newspaper, a brewery, even suburbs called Mormon Town, Maiden Town and Happy-Go-Lucky. Everything depended on gold and a great deal

of it depended on one mine, the famous Long Tunnel. It was a deep quartz mine, worked by machinery which was dragged into the mountains by horse and bullock teams. The Long Tunnel lasted fifty years and paid five million pounds in dividends to its shareholders. For the hundreds of men who worked the mine, the rewards were not so glittering. Six days a week underground in a world of shafts and cages and machinery and dust. It was a living, three pounds a week, but it was not the happy-go-lucky life of the digger.

Long Tunnel Mine, Walhalla

The men recognised their changed circumstances and sang ironic songs about the daily treadmill of mining:

> *The miner he goes and changes his clothes*
> *And then makes his way to the shaft*
> *For each man well knows he's going below*
> *To put in eight hours of graft.*
>
> *With his calico cap and his old flannel shirt*
> *His pants with the strap round the knee*
> *His boots watertight and his candle alight*
> *His crib and his billy of tea.*

*Underground miners
hauling timber*

*The tapman to the driver will knock four and one
The ropes to the windlass will strain
As one shift comes up, another goes down
And working commences again!*

*He works hard for his pay at six bob a day
He toils for his missus and kids
He gets what's left over and thinks he's in clover
To cut off his baccy from quids.*

*And thus he goes on, week in and week out
To toil for his life's daily bread
He's off to the mine, come hail, rain or shine
That his dear ones at home may be fed.*

*Diggin' holes in the ground where there's gold to be
        found
And most times where gold it is not
A man's like a rabbit with this diggin' habit
And like one he ought to be shot.*

More and more the scale of gold mining dwarfed the indi-

FOREST CREEK (VICTORIA) GOLD REEFS CRUSHING WORKS

The Garfield Wheel, Forest Creek, Castlemaine

vidual miner. The Garfield Wheel at Forest Creek, Castlemaine, was taller than a dozen miners standing on each other's shoulders. It was the biggest waterwheel in the southern hemisphere, and the timber frame took nearly a minute to make one revolution. Daring boys would straddle the spokes and ride it around like a giant ferris wheel, hanging on like grim death as they pointed downwards.

The Wheel supplied the power for a fifteen-head stamper battery which crushed massive amounts of ore from the Madam Garfield mine. But all this power was regulated by just one man with a brake lever to control the wheel. Machinery was taking over from the quarter of a million men who once swarmed the Victorian diggings.

Of course it took men to install the machinery and build the structures that were needed at the mines, like the massive flumes that carried the water to the waterwheels. It also took money, more than the men on the fields had. It was company money, raised from investors often as far away as London. And their interests came ahead of hired labour. Many diggers resented this new world. They had tasted freedom, and they would rush to new fields and starve rather than become company slaves. They didn't give up the *old* fields without a struggle.

The oldest Victorian goldfield, Clunes, was also the first field to witness big company operations. The Port Phillip and Colonial Gold Mining Company of London opened their Clunes mine in 1857 on private land they leased from a grazier.

A Swedish model-maker on the goldfields, Carl Nordstrom, made a model for the company in 1858. It showed all the operations involved in Australia's first deep quartz goldmine—the boiler house that supplied the steam power, the poppet head that held the winding wheels, the tunnels where the ore was mined, the shafts where it was drawn up to the surface, and the teams that carried it to the battery for crushing and the chemical separation of gold . . . all the links in the expensive chain of processes required for efficient quartz mining, which the Port Phillip Company did very successfully to make a million pound profit.

The small diggers on the Clunes field were not concerned about company efficiency, but about their own miners' rights. They said the company had far too much land, that it had no legal right to the gold (which it did not have under the laws of the time) and that it couldn't keep them out by fencing the land. They sank their shafts just outside the fence and then tunnelled right into the company's territory and got good alluvial gold. The company sank shafts into the invading tunnels and sent down their men, the Insiders, and there was a tremendous pitched battle underground, when the Insiders met the Outsiders.

The battle of Clunes was a draw at the time, but the company won in the long run, because the alluvial gold gave out and independent diggers just couldn't finance their own quartz mines. Company mining was the wave of the future, and the Golden Age was just beginning for the money manager and the shrewd investor. Australia was soon to see its first mining millionaires.

JB Watson of Bendigo boasted of buying a fifty-shilling

share that was worth £10 000 a few years later. He did not make his million by being an easy mark. But he met his match in 1867 when Australia's first royal visitor, Prince Alfred, Duke of Edinburgh, came to Bendigo. There he cracked out a few bits of quartz and then was feasted 121 metres below ground. The banquet room was carved out of the rock, and the floors were carpeted and the walls draped for the occasion.

The Prince was shown a display of the company's gold nuggets. It was thought he might even choose a small sample as a souvenir of his visit. But with the simplicity which is the mark of true breeding, the Prince pocketed all the most valuable nuggets—worth in today's money, about $100 000. Watson didn't say anything, probably because he was in shock, but he later told the press that the Prince had chosen 'rather freely'. Incidentally the name of the mine was the Great Hustler.

But the goldmines of Victoria could stand this trifling loss. In less than a century they produced nearly 3000 tons of gold, for a financial return of $760 million. Bendigo

Mullock heap, the New Australasian Mine, Creswick

alone produced 830 tons of gold. However, the workers in the quartz mines saw little of this wealth. Till the end of the century they only earned three pounds a week. They managed to get their working hours down from sixty a week to forty-eight, and they had a steady job, but conditions underground were grim. Because of the dust from machine drilling, miners' deaths from lung disease were six times the average Victorian rate and the Bendigo miner's life expectancy was just forty-five years.

The most tragic instance of the dangers of underground mining happened at the Victorian town of Creswick in December 1882. The New Australasian Mine was flooded when water from old workings burst into a new drive that was being opened by contractors. The water poured into the main washdirt drive with such force that the wind currents blew the candles out. Twenty-seven miners were unable to escape up the shaft and were trapped below in the darkness. The men huddled in the jump-ups along the side of the tunnel and they prayed and sang the hymn 'In the Sweet Bye and Bye' as the water rose around them. On

the surface there were heart-rending scenes when the
water was pumped out and the miners' families saw the
bodies brought up. Five men miraculously survived but
twenty-two suffocated or drowned in Australia's worst
gold mining disaster.

*Destruction of the
picturesque*

At Creswick today only a mullock heap marks the site
of that tragedy and the location of the New Australasian
Mine. This is not untypical of Australian gold mining history. In some cases it is not just the goldmines that have
disappeared, but virtually the entire towns they supported.

There is little at Hill End today to indicate that it was once
the richest goldfield in New South Wales. The few buildings that remain have not changed much in a century. The
startling change is in what is no longer there. The now
peaceful paddocks above the Turon River north of Bathurst were for a short time the home of the biggest inland
town in New South Wales.

Hill End in its boom year of 1872 was a roaring gold

Crowded poppet head

town with 8000 people crowded into its narrow allotments and 40 000 people in the surrounding district. The main street, Clarke Street, was a continuous line of shops and hotels for a kilometre and a half. Hill End township had twenty-eight pubs, three banks, numerous churches. Real estate values were sky-high, and Smith's Cheapjack Tobacco Warehouse had to operate with a street frontage of just over two metres.

But the real business end of Hill End was the incredible jumble of whims and shafts and mullock heaps and stampers called Hawkins Hill. Around 1870 the rich reefs of Hawkins Hill began to produce record yields of gold from ore. One stamping of twenty tons of rock produced 1200 ounces of gold. The field was called the Golden Quartermile and it became a rabbit warren of 120 mines worked by thousands of men.

The most notable of the Hawkins Hill mines was the Star of Hope. In 1872 this mine produced the biggest piece of golden rock ever found in the world. It was so heavy that it took twelve miners with crowbars to lever it to the top of the ridge. The Star of Hope mine and its manager, Bernard Holtermann, won instant fame through this remarkable find, which was soon known far and wide as Holtermann's Nugget.

In fact it was not a nugget, but a huge slab of quartz and slate, one and a half metres high, half a metre wide and shot through with reef gold which crushed out at over 3000 ounces. And it wasn't Holtermann's. He was not there when it was found, and he didn't personally own it. But he had a photograph made which combined his picture and a separate picture of the lump of gold to make it look as if the two of them were very close acquaintances. Holtermann used this photo in an advertising poster for his Life Preserving Drops. Only one copy of this poster remains and it is in a very appropriate place, surveying the bar of Hill End's Royal Hotel, where many an old gold-miner has come to take a medicinal drop or two.

The late nineteenth century was the great age of patent

Above: *Royal Hotel, Hill End*
Top right: *Golden Gully, Hill End*
Bottom right: *Gold Assay Office, Hill End*

Holtermann without nugget

medicines, especially on the goldfields where doctors were scarce and genuine doctors even scarcer. For any complaint there was an appropriate price, but Holtermann thought big. His Life Preserving Drops promised to cure practically any complaint you could think of, from leprosy to ringworm. History has dispensed with the Life Preserving Drops, but the legend of Bernard Holtermann lives on. He was one of those remarkable figures that flashed like a meteor across the Australian skies in the Golden Age.

Born in Hamburg, Germany, Holtermann was infected by the gold rush fever of the 1850s and came to Australia to seek his fortune. He found his way to Hill End and teamed up with a Polish digger, Louis Beyers, in gold mining, storekeeping and other commercial ventures. One of Holtermann's abiding interests was photography and it is because of his passion for the camera that we know as much as we do about life on the Australian goldfields.

Weight : 630 lbs
Height : 4ft 9m
Width : 2ft 2m
Average thickness 4 inches
Value £12000

Holtermann commissioned the talented photographer, Beaufoy Merlin, to make a record of Hill End and its citizens in 1872. The result was an unparalleled documentary record of an Australian gold town in its golden year. The miners of Hill End, their wives and families, probably thought that they were there to stay. Their houses were modest, but neat and well cared for, often with little gardens. Their faces radiated a certain pride. They hoped for better things for themselves and their children, and in 1872 they had every right to expect that Hill End would make it happen. But within a few years Hill End stopped happening. The gold started to give out, confidence gave out even faster and the people packed their traps and went in search of newer pastures and greener fields.

Holtermann himself transferred to Sydney in 1875, but he had done well enough from Hill End gold to build an imposing mansion on the North Shore—it was later incor-

Holtermann's house, Sydney

porated into the school now known as Shore. Holtermann continued to busy himself with many enterprises. He was a lively and public-spirited citizen of Sydney, became a Member of Parliament, and proposed many ideas which were somewhat ahead of his time. He retained his zeal for photography and the tower of his house was in fact the world's largest tripod, expressly built to photograph panoramic views of Sydney.

Holtermann was a tireless salesman for his adopted country and a believer in the saying that a picture was worth a thousand words. He employed Beaufoy Merlin and then Charles Bayliss on the camera, and later took his vast photographic collection overseas, at his own expense, to advertise Sydney and New South Wales. His photo collections were highlights of the Philadelphia Centennial Exhibition of 1876 and the Paris *Exposition Universelle* of 1878. They made many people aware of the remarkable development of the remote continent down under.

By the 1870s the majority of Australian people were native-born. By the 1880s they were confident and even boastful about their progress and their prospects. They were still a collection of six colonies, and not yet one nation, but many of them believed that they had advanced more rapidly in a shorter time than any country on the earth. They had self government, manhood suffrage, the secret ballot and the eight-hour day. Gold towns might rise and burst like bubbles, but exports of wool and gold were earning Australia a handsome living.

There was full employment and general prosperity, increasingly reflected in the capitals where trade was centred. Sydney had risen from its unpromising beginnings as a convict prison to a gracious city of a quarter of a million people. Working conditions for men and women were harsh by our standards, but not by the standards of that time. An endless flow of immigrants from the Old World felt they had arrived in the paradise of the common people, and the native-born reflected on their luck at being able to enjoy the climate, the leisure and indeed the beauty of such a city.

The optimism that had begun with the great gold strikes of the 1850s continued in Australia for the next forty years of the Golden Age and became almost an ingrained characteristic of the Australian people. They had seen depressions and hard times before, but now it seemed that the wealth of the country was unbounded. The good times would roll on and the future would keep getting better. Utopia looked to be just around the corner and there was no reason to believe it was not. Just occasionally confidence was jolted by a warning shot, fired at a place such as Hill End.

It was a simple trick to load the muzzle of a shotgun with pellets of gold and fire it into the rock face of a mine. A bucket of water thrown over the face of the rock, and lo, the glittering gold appeared. And it looked like there was plenty more where that came from. But for every genuine goldmine floated at Hill End, another was a dud. The rogues who thrived on the business of share speculation had built the technique of salting mines into a fine art.

The investors in many cases did not have *their* business down to a fine art. They were rank amateurs, easy meat for sharp company promoters who floated so many Hill End mines that the Sydney Stock Exchange was formed.

Shares in the new mines were usually fully taken up within forty-eight hours, and one of the trademarks of the Golden Age was a growing pile of handsome but utterly worthless shares in fraudulent gold mines.

Bernard Holtermann knew what was going on at Hill End, and he made himself thoroughly unpopular in that town—in fact, he was burnt in effigy there by a big crowd—because he warned Sydney investors to check up on Hill End goldmines before they invested in them. Other people also knew that funny games were being played and they tried to warn the gullible. In the *Sydney Morning Herald* of March 7, 1872, amidst a welter of genuine prospectuses for more or less genuine Hill End mines, there appeared a savagely satirical advertisement:

THE GIGANTIC BAMBOOZLE GOLD, TIN AND COPPER MINING CO. LTD. OF VULTURES HILL

Capital £500,000 in £1 shares
Promoters Shares: 250,000 with £20,000 in cash
Subscribers Shares: 250,000
Directors: Tigg Montague, Uriah Heep,
Noah Claypole, Chevy Slyme,
Potstausend Donnerwetter, Olly Pecksniff
Brokers: Catchum Quick, Nabbum & Co.
The Devils Chambers
Bottomless-pit Street

The promoters of this company having discovered *a rich gold mine in Sydney* are deeply impressed with the necessity of working same to their own advantage with all convenient speed. To this end they propose working the property on the system known as the

FOUR PEG SYSTEM

which has been most profitably worked in Victoria, New Zealand and elsewhere. Their motives are of the highest character and may be expressed in those undying words:

HEADS WE WIN, TAILS YOU LOSE.

For the pegs, which are made of the finest timber they could get, the promoters ask the modest sum of £5000 each. They further propose to dig a hole to see if there is anything in the ground but the pegs. The directors announce their intention of making all the calls until the ground is thoroughly proved, or at all events until

THEY HAVE GOT RID OF THEIR SHARES.

Under the company laws of that day, it really was a Heads We Win, Tails You Lose situation for many investors. They could be called on to keep subscribing money, but the company directors were free to sell out their shares at the best profit before the investors discovered that the mine had no gold, was not even pegged out, or did not even exist.

And so many a small businessman and suburban widow lost their little nest eggs on Hill End mines. But they were not the last Australians to burn their fingers in the share market in the quest for the quick quid, and they were not utter fools. They believed there was still plenty of gold in the Australian earth. And in that, at least, they were right.

Down in Bendigo stock exchanges were buzzing like beehives with speculation in gold mines which were making, in many cases, genuine profits. Banks displayed in their windows cakes of gold retorted from Bendigo mines. Shares were traded all day and till 2 am and young and old, respectable and disreputable, played the share market as we might play poker machines. Anthony Trollope watched the dealers at work and said he trembled 'lest his eyes should be picked out of his head' as he passed by.

Up north in Queensland there were new and almost unbelievable prospects like the Ironstone Mountain, inland from Rockhampton. Opened up by the Morgan brothers in 1882 and rechristened Mount Morgan, it proved to be a veritable mountain of gold and it returned amazing riches for every ton of ironstone that was crushed.

Of all the lucky strikes in that Golden Age, Mount Morgan has to be rated Number One. Eighteen companies mined on its perimeters and got nothing, but the riches of the mountain itself went on and on, gold and silver and copper, for nearly a century, until a mountain became a hole in the ground, the Glory Hole, big enough to hold the waters of Sydney Harbour.

It was the longest-lived metal mine in Australia, the richest single goldmine in the world and only goldmine where the lion's share of the wealth went to a tiny handful of men who held the shares. The original shareholders in the Mount Morgan mine, six men, put in an investment of £2000. That was all they ever had to find. From then on the mine paid for itself 550 times over. The Morgan brothers sold out their shares after two years and thought they'd reaped a handsome profit, but little did they know how

The Customs House, Quay Street, Rockhampton

much gold was left.

The men who ended up as major shareholders were Walter Hall, whose millions eventually were bequeathed to Australian charities, and William Knox D'Arcy, a lucky Rockhampton lawyer who was invited to contribute £500 to the original syndicate.

D'Arcy ended up with at least one third of the Mount Morgan shares, became Australia's richest man and did not leave any of the dividends to Australian charities. He took the loot to England where he bought a mansion in London and two country estates and the only private box at Ascot, apart from the Royal Box. He had his dividends from Mount Morgan sent to him in gold bars. D'Arcy was another of those larger than life figures of the Golden Age. He invested his profits in prospecting oil leases in Persia and struck lucky again. His oil company eventually became British Petroleum—BP—a giant enterprise founded on Australian gold.

Perhaps the place that least reflects the fortunes won out of the Mount Morgan Mine by D'Arcy and his colleagues

is Mount Morgan itself. It was a working miners' town and it still looks just like that.

Rockhampton is a different story. It was the port through which the wealth of the Mount Morgan Mines flowed, and a good portion of it stuck. Quay Street, Rockhampton, is one of the most magnificent streets in Australia. Nearly all the buildings were erected in the 1880s and 1890s when all exports from the region were carried away from the wharves on the Fitzroy River after clearing through the Customs House.

In time the railways came, the river silted up and there is not much to be seen now of Rockhampton's original wharves. But the Quay Street buildings express what the Golden Age meant to Australia, how the wealth was displayed. And many of them have a direct relation to the

Mount Morgan Mine. Avonleigh was the townhouse of Frederick Morgan. The Technical and Further Education Offices were built for Hall and D'Arcy. The Goldsbrough Mort building was built for the Halls. The ABC Building, no longer renowned for its wealth, was once the Mount Morgan Gold Mining Company offices. They held their board meetings there, and stored their gold bullion there before transhipping it to the Queen's Wharf. And D'Arcy had his office in the building named, very appropriately, Luck House. The original Morgan Gold Mining Company paid dividends of eleven million pounds on the investment of £2000.

Meanwhile other Queensland goldfields, hungry for investment, reaped a rich new field of speculation—the London market. The Colonial and Indian Exhibition was staged in London in 1886 and drew five million spectators. One of the most popular displays was a stamper battery crushing a hundred tons of ore from the mines of Charters Towers in North Queensland. The effect of this display was reinforced by the spectacle of a huge cake of retorted gold from the mines, and by frequent cables from Charters Towers telling of rich dividends and promising new fields. When Charters Towers shares were floated in London, British investors fell on them in droves, paying up to twenty times their original worth.

It was not just the British public who were hypnotised by the stamping process. Great machines like the Venus Battery at Charters Towers had extended the Golden Age in Australia by many years. Long after the richest deposits of alluvial gold were exhausted, the stampers continued to produce fortunes by their capacity to crush payable gold out of vast quantities of quartz rock. These machines themselves were seen as the instruments of prosperity, objects fit for the adoration of the Australian people.

> *I'm sure there's no melody equalled on earth*
> *No instrument ever yet seen*
> *So full of light music and exquisite mirth*
> *As the good old quartz crushing machine.*
>
> *The stampers are pounding away at the stone*
> *To make it its treasure unfold*
> *Till at last the result of its labour is shown*
> *In a cake of bright beautiful gold.*

So hurrah for the greatest invention on earth
On whose labours all industries lean
The cradle where all kind of wealth has its birth
The good old quartz crushing machine!

Charters Towers was the cradle of North Queensland's wealth and the main force in the development of that whole region. Discovered on Christmas Eve 1871 by Jupiter, an Aboriginal boy who'd gone in search of prospector Hugh Mosman's lost horse and found a creek glittering with gold nuggets, Charters Towers was soon rushed by thousands of alluvial miners. But its true wealth was found to be in deep quartz reefs. Famous Charters Towers mines like the Day Dawn and the Brilliant produced enough gold to make it the fourth richest field in Australian history.

Charters Towers became Queensland's biggest city outside Brisbane. Its residents considered it superior to Brisbane and, indeed, to anywhere else. They felt that Charters Towers had so much of everything life could offer that they called it quite simply 'The World'. In the warm North Queensland nights the main streets were sometimes so thronged with people that they had to be closed to traffic.

The various stock exchanges of Charters Towers were centralised in 1890 in the Royal Arcade. Inside the Stock Exchange it was all go. Three calls a day with the night call open to the public and the galleries packed with speculators following the mines' fortunes and their own. Rumour galloped upon rumour. The Day Dawn Block had a promising new formation. Up went the shares. Buy at any price! But unluckily the formation had wedged out. Down went the shares. Sell at any price! Rich men lost their shirts and poor men became tycoons in one night's gambling.

The gold was there and the money followed it. Charters Towers was so strong financially that it pulled the whole State out of a crisis and it was so confident that it advertised itself to Melbourne investors as:

Gold, Nothing but Gold
The Greatest Gold City in the World.

There were other cities in Australia prepared to dispute that title—Ballarat for one. Ballarat was the richest alluvial goldfield ever discovered. By 1853, just two years after it started, it had produced more than all the gold mined in California to that time. The total production of the Ballarat

Ballarat City Hall and statue of Queen Victoria

field eventually exceeded 750 tons of gold. This enormous wealth was reflected in such institutions of the city as the Ballarat City Hall, the Railway Station and the Cathedral of St Patrick.

Even those other cathedrals of the people, the pubs, expressed the magnificent optimism of the Golden Age. The Golden City Hotel was perhaps the most charming of the 477 hotels in the Ballarat district. The most impressive was undoubtedly Craig's Hotel. Here was no mean shanty town, no fly-by-night canvas town. Here was a city built to last for centuries.

The wealth of the New South Wales goldfields was trifling by comparison with Victoria's but the city of Bathurst also has its treasures from the Golden Age, including one of

The Court House, Bathurst

Australia's best public buildings from that period. The Bathurst Court House was designed by the Government Architect, James Barnet, and its elegant portico, its turreted dome and its sweeping colonnades still grace the centre of Bathurst a century later.

Bathurst had its share of fine private houses too, and one of them housed a giant of the Golden Age. Hereford, across the Macquarie River from Bathurst, was built in 1880 as the residence of James Rutherford, an American who had come to the Australian gold rushes on an impulse. He had been planning to sail from New York to California but changed his mind and caught a ship to Melbourne. He found his fortune, not as a digger, but as the boss of the biggest coachline network in the world, Cobb and Co.

The founder of this coaching line was Freeman Cobb. With three other young Americans, he started a service between Port Melbourne and Melbourne in 1853 and expanded the service the next year to the goldfields of

139

Cobb & Co, Bourke Street, Melbourne

Castlemaine, Bendigo and Ballarat. Cobb and Co quickly won golden opinions in Victoria for their speedy and efficient service and the comfort of their Concord coaches. The coaches were at first imported from America, but soon they were being made in Australia and their dashing American drivers were joined by Australian coachmen.

Legendary drivers like the Tasmanian-born Cabbage Tree Ned Devine became the kings of the Australian roads in the nineteenth century. Cabbage Tree Ned drove the first English cricket team to tour Australia in 1862. He is also said to have driven the biggest stagecoach in the world, the Great Leviathan. Built in Ballarat in 1859 it was pulled by a team of twenty-two greys and carried some eighty passengers.

Cobb and Co had four changes of ownership before James Rutherford took over the firm in 1861. The railways were expanding from Melbourne to Ballarat and Bendigo and Rutherford made a bold decision to shift the whole enterprise overland from Victoria to Bathurst. The day the great cavalcade arrived in Bathurst in June 1862, with

Rutherford himself driving the lead coach, was recorded as a red-letter event by the *Bathurst Free Press:*

> On Thursday the town of Bathurst was pleasantly excited by the arrival of the coaching plant of Cobb and Co. of Melbourne. It was like the triumphant entrance of a first class equestrian troupe on a heavy scale. There were eight comfortably covered company coaches horsed by 52 high-mettled and well-trained roadsters, driven by bearded and moustached 'whips', apparently of no mean stamp. Six of the teams comprised respectively seven dashing animals, which were handled with less seeming anxiety than one of our own 'towneys' would manage his tandem turn-out. Had a band of music preceded the 'line' the town might have 'hailed' for a half-holiday.

From its Bathurst headquarters Cobb and Co extended into the far hinterlands of New South Wales and Queensland. By the 1870s it was harnessing 6000 horses a day. By the 1880s its coachlines covered eastern Australia from Cooktown and Normanton down to Melbourne, and from the east coast to west of the Darling.

It had become the most extensive coaching network in the world and a major bush industry employing a legion of drivers and coach builders, harness-makers and stable hands and depot clerks, and supporting hundreds of hostelries and eating houses on its stage lines through the vast back country. The company had a bold motto. 'We Lead. Those Who Can May Follow.' But few could follow the Cobb and Co coaches in the early days because they were designed to travel to remote goldfields and bush outposts where no roads existed.

The cabins of the Cobb and Co coaches were supported underneath by leather straps which cushioned the passengers from the dreadful jolting of the older English coaches on their steel springs. However, the leather brace system made the cabin rock forwards and backwards, and passengers were inclined to get seasick. One English lady recorded that she was about to faint when the lady next to her fainted instead. This event, she said, somewhat restored her spirits.

It was a highly democratic form of travel. Everybody had to endure the same discomfort and overcrowding and the same dangers from bushrangers who stuck up thirty-six Cobb and Co coaches for their gold. There were very few accidents, which was a great tribute to the skill of the drivers, but lots of coaches got bogged and when they did everyone but women and children had to get out and push.

Like the gold diggers themselves, Cobb and Co traversed Australia from the snow-clad mountains to the northern jungles to the far western plains. It became the legend of the bush that Cobb and Co would always get through. As Henry Lawson recalled, the bush dwellers knew no greater thrill than the clatter of hooves, the jingle of harness, the shouts of the driver, the snorting of the spendid thorough-breds, the crack of the whips and the blast of the bugle that signalled the arrival of Cobb and Co.

> *The roaring camps of Gulgong, and many a Digger's Rest*
> *The diggers on the Lachlan; the huts of Farthest West*
> *Some thirty thousand exiles who sailed for weal or woe*
> *The bravest hearts of twenty lands will wait for Cobb and Co.*
>
> *Swift scramble up the sidling, where teams climb inch by inch*
> *Pause bird-like on the summit—then breakneck down the pinch*
> *By clear ridge-country rivers, and gaps where tracks run high*
> *Where waits the lonely horseman, cut clear against the sky;*
> *Past haunted halfway houses—where convicts made the bricks—*
> *Scrub-yards and new bark shanties, we dash with five and six;*
> *Through stringybark and bluegum, and box and pine we go—*
> *A hundred miles shall see tonight the lights of Cobb and Co.*

There was a rival, a slow giant pursuing Cobb and Co. A great edifice at Maryborough in Victoria led Mark Twain to describe Maryborough as 'a railway station with a town attached'. It might have looked like that, but the truth was that the town had come first. When the gold rush started in 1851 nobody knew how long any of the goldfields might last. Ten years later it was clear that some of the inland settlements were there to stay. Then the railways began to funnel out from the capital cities to the new centres of prosperity.

The Railway Station,
Maryborough

Australia's entry into the railway age was not particularly dramatic. The first train ran in 1854 from Melbourne to Port Melbourne, a distance of five kilometres. By 1861 Australia still had less than 500 kilometres of railway track. But this network was now reaching towards the key gold centres of Ballarat and Bendigo. Cobb and Co found itself pushed off these lucrative passenger and freight lines, and had to move further out.

Railway construction picked up pace. By 1881 Australia had nearly ten thousand kilometres of track. By 1891 it was over twenty thousand kilometres, and Brisbane, Sydney and Melbourne, the major east coast cities, were all linked by rail.

The gold of cities like Bendigo largely created the Australian Railway boom. Gold fetched the inland populations whose demands for goods and services and communications then fetched the railways. And gold created the confidence and the prosperity which made it

143

possible to borrow the large capital sums needed to build the railways.

None of this came as a surprise to Bendigo, which had always forecast a train of progress with itself in the leading van. Back in the 1850s it changed its name from Bendigo, the nickname of a bare knuckle prizefighter, to Sandhurst, after the English military academy. That high-toned new name led Charles Thatcher to some satirical reflections about the changes to old Bendigo:

> *Dear me! How this place is advancing*
> *What it will come to I'm sure I don't know*
> *The way folks are building is truly entrancing*
> *They've altered the fashion of old Bendigo*
> *Lands advertised every day for selection*
> *Quartz reefs still keep up their fabulous yield*
> *Brick houses spring up in every direction*
> *And canvas is beaten quite out of the field.*
>
> *Fine handsome shops everywhere are erected*
> *Where new goods from London and Paris you'll see*
> *But of course that is only what would be expected*
> *For ladies will go it to get finery*
> *Jackson will tempt 'em as much as he's able*
> *And tries hard to sell 'em a splendid silk dress*
> *And Francis allures them with his shilling tables*
> *Walking into their purses with splendid success.*
>
> *But of course now on Sandhurst, we go on improving*
> *In the great march of progress we're first in the race*
> *Our motto of course is just push on, keep moving*
> *For Bendigo's bound to become a great place.*

Actually the Bendigonians were never keen on the name of Sandhurst, as the British military were not too popular on the goldfields after Eureka Stockade. In due course, they changed the name back to Bendigo. But Thatcher was right in his predictions. It *was* bound to become a great place. Before the end of the century it was calling itself the Paris of the New World, and Thatcher would have been hard put to recognise the magnificent Shamrock Hotel as the noisy smoky music hall where he'd once entertained the diggers with his topical ballads.

As you'd expect from the name, the Shamrock Hotel was founded by Irishmen, Billy Heffernan and John Crowley, and it did so well from the money the diggers spent on grog and the gold dust that their boots left on the bar-room floor that it was replaced by a second and grander hotel, and that was eventually replaced by a third and even grander Shamrock. Every famous visitor to Bendigo stayed at the Shamrock, from royalty to the only survivor of the Burke and Wills expedition, and a host of theatricals like J C Williamson, Maggie Moore and Nellie Stewart.

A crowd of ten thousand people gathered outside to salute Mademoiselle Ilma de Murska, the Hungarian Nightingale, after her theatre performance, and they would not go home till she consented to sing 'The Last Rose of Summer' from the balcony, leaving not a dry eye in the entire street.

Dame Nellie Melba stayed in one of the front suites. The story that she had the nearby Post Office clock stopped from chiming the quarter hours at night because it ruined her sleep is denied by the management, but it is not surprising that the legend should have arisen. The Shamrock was a place that created legends. It was the Mecca of the high-steppers and the big spenders in Bendigo's golden age and if any man struck it rich, the locals had the saying: 'He'll dine at the Shamrock tonight'.

In Bendigo's Pall Mall is the statue of a man who could have dined at the Shamrock every night if he chose. He struck it very rich indeed, and became legendary in Australian mining history as the Quartz King of Bendigo.

George Lansell came from England to Bendigo in the 1850s rush. He was smart enough to see better ways of getting gold than digging it up himself, and he combined with his brothers in a tallow factory. He invested his profits in quartz mines and lost the lot, saved up again and lost it all again. Then he plunged again and it was third time lucky. Lansell's investments in the Advance Company and the Cinderella Mine paid off handsomely. Unlike other speculators Lansell did not take the money and run. Against the conventional wisdom of the time he believed that Bendigo's gold went very deep into the ground. He backed this hunch with his own money and it paid him a fortune and started the practice of very deep mining in Australia.

The Bendigo goldfield became known as Quartzopolis, thirteen square kilometres of brick chimneys belching smoke, steam engine sheds, stamper batteries and a forest of 200 poppet heads. Under them were the deepest gold-

Above left: *The Central Deborah Mine, Bendigo*
Above right: *Shamrock Hotel, Bendigo*

mines in the world. Much of this was due to Lansell. He installed the world's biggest stamper at Bendigo—105 head. He owned nine of the mines personally and was director of some forty more, and he led by example, continually investing his capital in better mining machinery and technology.

Previously quartz mining operated by a hit or miss method of sinking shafts to see if there was gold. Lansell was chiefly responsible for the introduction of the diamond drill, which could bring up core samples from deep underground and establish if a shaft was worth sinking. This was a first for Australia in 1880 and Bendigo sang a boastful song about the diamond drill, recommending it to other less enlightened mining fields of Australia.

> *Well, the diamond drill is all the go*
> *'Twill work a platte or reef, sir*
> *Five hundred feet is nothing now*
> *It passes all belief, sir*
>
> *True, a rod may break sometimes*
> *A most confounded bore, sir*
> *But tried in South Australia*
> *'Twill prove true to the core, sir.*

Above left: *George Lansell by Longstaff*
Above right: *The diamond drill*

Lansell was popular in Bendigo because he had go-ahead ideas and faith in the mines which he backed up with money. But the man had his enemies and one morning he discovered an empty coffin had been left in his backyard. Perhaps he took this as a threat on his life. He went to London and spent the next seven years there, until he received a remarkable document from Bendigo in 1887.

It was a scroll signed by 2628 prominent citizens of Bendigo and it petitioned George Lansell to return to the city which needed him so much. He did return. The *Annals of Bendigo* said:

> The true grit in the man and his unbounded faith in the district would not let him abandon the search for the elusive yellow metal ... The Australian Quartz King stands pre-eminent amongst all our mining men for pluck and enterprise.

He brought back the golden touch with him. The gold mines, which had been in the doldrums, boomed again, while fortune smiled on George Lansell as kindly as ever. His mansion, Fortuna, was a landmark of Bendigo. Built on top of the New Chum Reef and within earshot of the stamper battery and the steam engines of the 180, Lansell's richest and best-loved mine, Fortuna was a powerful symbol of the great gambles that paid off in the golden age.

The story of Fortuna is the story of the luck, but also of the shrewdness and daring that made Lansell a millionaire. The previous owner of the house and the 180 mine next door was a German named Ballerstedt. He had made a lot of the money from the 180 and thought the gold was finished, so he was pleased to sell the mine and the house to Lansell for a handsome sum—£30 000. But even before Ballerstedt got off the ship that took him home to Germany, the news was out that Lansell had gone deeper and found a new reef worth £180 000—six times what he had paid for the house and mine.

It must have been golden music to Lansell's ears to hear the 180 mine, the prime source of his fortunes, rumbling and stamping away just outside his house. Most of his money was re-invested in Bendigo mines, a good deal of it went to Bendigo charities, the rest was spent on Fortuna. Lansell kept adding on to Fortuna until it was a grand and ornate mansion of forty-one rooms and three storeys, surrounded by beautiful parklands and gardens, ornamental lakes and fountains.

Fortuna was the complete rich man's castle—it had everything, ballrooms, music rooms, observatories, libraries, drawing rooms, picture galleries, billiard rooms, swimming pools and gymnasium. The interior was packed with antique English furniture, French paintings, statues, Japanese bronzes, rare crystal—all the expensive trappings which the Lansells collected on their overseas trips. But the stained glass windows expressed an Australian note, cheery and optimistic, as if to say that Australia advanced at the same rate as Fortuna in these golden years.

No Australian city seemed to justify feelings of confidence more than Melbourne. Half a century after it began as a settlement called Bearbrass, consisting of a dozen bark huts, it had become the most magnificent of Australian cities. The wealth of Victorian gold had transformed it into a dynamic metropolis, bigger than Sydney, bigger than San Francisco, and the undisputed financial capital of Australia.

Visitors to Melbourne were astonished by the progress of the city, and the splendours of Collins Street, the street of banking places and golden dreams. The citizens were described as 'a go-ahead self-confident Yankee sort of people'. An English journalist, Francis Adams, observed: 'Melbourne is the phenomenal city of Australia, and its people have in it a pride which is a passion.'

Another English journalist, George Augustus Sala, dubbed it 'Marvellous Melbourne'. The name caught on and was repeated with relish by the Melbourne people. They believed the truth of the phrase was self-evident. Almost overnight Melbourne had flowered into a great world city, and it was still advancing on every front. It was a great port city, a great railway city, it had tramways and electric lighting, rapidly expanding suburbs to house the children of the gold rush generation, and a vigorous artistic and theatrical life. Its people felt the excitement of living in the stirring age of a boom city where progress was visible and swift.

Did not the Melbourne *Age* have the biggest newspaper circulation in the Southern Hemisphere? Did not the Victorian Public Library have the biggest dome in the Southern Hemisphere? Was not the Melbourne Cup Day already established as *the* day of the year in the Australian sporting calendar? And was not the Melbourne code of Australian Rules football the finest game ever invented?

The spectacles of Marvellous Melbourne astonished all eyes. Here was a city which delighted in its wealth. True, there were slums and industrial suburbs like seething rabbit warrens, but the luckier citizens averted their eyes from the slums, while they strolled the fashionable Block along Collins and Swanston Streets.

The whole city exhibited its wealth and finery at a grand International Exhibition in 1880, and an even grander Centennial Exhibition in 1888. Just one century after the arrival of the first white settler in Australia, Melbourne staged this great spectacle in its Exhibition Building.

The Exhibition Building stands today as one of the great monuments of the Golden Age in all its wealth and pride, surrounded by the extensive and beautiful parks and gardens which also became the trademarks of this gold rush city. As they gazed upon the Parliament and the Treasury buildings and the massive Law Courts and the churches and cathedrals of Melbourne, old-time diggers might have recalled those lines from Thatcher's song, 'Look Out Below':

> *Wherever he turned his wandering eyes*
> *Great wealth he did behold*
> *And peace and plenty hand in hand*
> *By the magic power of gold.*

Government House, Melbourne, was spoken of as the finest house in the land. Melbourne's theatres, like the Princess Theatre, revealed an increasing and almost frenzied urge to decorate and elaborate and spend money. And the banks, the lynchpin of the financial capital, were not to be outdone in this conspicuous display of wealth. The temples of the moneychangers reached their pinnacle of luxury in the Gothic Bank of the ES&A built in Collins Street in 1887.

Master craftsmen were brought in to decorate the building and no expense was spared. The extravagance reached its height in the lofty ceiling of the banking chamber. Above the cast iron columns and the arches, the ceiling was decorated with thousands of sheets of hand-beaten gold leaf—so much gold, it was said, that if joined together in one inch-wide strip, it would reach right around the world at the equator.

It was a Golden Age in more ways than one. Gold was always in public use and in the public eye. Men carried gold watches and chains and cigarette cases, women wore a lot of gold jewellery, wages were paid in gold sovereigns. So perhaps the Gothic Bank's golden ceiling didn't seem so extravagant at the time.

But all this glitter was based on something less substantial than gold. Mining speculation was overtaken in the 1880s by land speculation and the Melbourne banks led the way. The ES&A were able to build the Gothic Bank because they sold the Collins Street block next door for twice what they'd paid for it a short time before. Collins Street real estate was changing hands faster than gold sovereigns, at prices that would not be seen again for fifty years. For this great bubble was puffed up by British capital, bor-

Above left: *'Fortuna',
Bendigo*
Above right: *Window at
'Fortuna'*

Above left: *Parliament House, Melbourne*
Above right: *Exhibition Building, Melbourne*

rowed recklessly by the banks and misused in real estate gambling. A trade recession in 1890, falling prices for Australian exports, and British investors' decisions to recall their money—and suddenly the bubble burst, and Marvellous Melbourne fell like Lucifer.

Proud and mighty men like James Munro, Premier of Victoria in 1890, came tumbling down. Munro was a temperance man, a wowser, who invested the funds of his bank and his building society in non-alcoholic coffee palaces like the Grand, now the Windsor Hotel.

Somehow he was able to fence off his puritanical morals from his financial ethics. When he saw the crunch coming, he rushed laws through Parliament which were intended to allow banks and building societies to wind themselves up without paying their creditors. Then Munro appointed himself Agent-General in London and 'skedaddled'. Eventually he was forced to return and face bitter music.

> *Marvellous Melbourne, once so grand,*
> *Is humbled now quite out of hand*
> *Her money spent in buying land*
> *At prices far too good to stand*
> *The boom is dead you'll understand*
> *It is in short a failure grand*
> *The boom's decayed, it fades away*
> *And we all sing ta-ra-land-boom-de-ay.*

No part of Melbourne considered itself so marvellous as Toorak, the byword for wealth, exclusivity and snobbery. No boom mansion in Toorak was more marvelled at than Illawarra, the residence of Charles Henry James, a grocer from North Melbourne who subdivided land in the new suburbs which were springing up like mushrooms beside the railway tracks.

There is something about the house with its mad tower that expresses a final frenzied spasm of action just before a cardiac arrest. It was all done with other people's money, of course, and James collapsed with the rest in the 1890s. But he had taken the precaution of putting his entire estate in his wife's name. His creditors couldn't get their hands on Illawarra and they had to accept six pence three farthings in the pound on debts of nearly a million pounds.

The money men of Melbourne acted in the crash according to their own basic natures. Quite a few managed to hide away their real assets, pay off a tiny fraction of their debts, and re-emerge in later years as 'gentlemen' of Toorak. Financiers with a shade more conscience took poison, shot themselves or in some cases walked straight into the Yarra River and drowned themselves.

But most of the victims were little people. Not just the small investors who had all their savings gambled away by crooked directors of banks and building societies, but the hundreds of thousands who were thrown out of work when the banks collapsed like dominoes. Business stopped, public works stopped, private building stopped, all those jobs disappeared and Victoria lost population for the first time in its history. The shock waves spread through Australia and the blithe optimism of forty years of gold vanished like a dream.

It was not the end of Australian gold—that was to rise again in the West and restore Australia's fortunes for the start of the new century. But it was the end of that rich harvest of civilisation which sprang from the wealth of the eastern goldfields and which left us so many indelible monuments to a Golden Age of Australian optimism.

Land of Gold

The 'Song of Australia' written by Carl Linger and Mrs CJ Carleton in 1860 never became the national anthem, but it could certainly have served as the gold diggers' anthem:

> *There is a land where treasures shine*
> *Deep in the dark unfathomed mine*
> *For worshippers at Mammon's shrine*
> *Where gold lies hid and rubies gleam*
> *And fabled wealth no more doth seem*
> *The idle fancy of a dream.*
> *Australia, Australia, Australia.*

Australia, the land of gold, drew the gold seekers into wild and desperate places like Kiandra in the Snowy Mountains, the highest goldfield in the country. Surviving the winter there was as big a challenge as finding the gold. But it was not just to worship at Mammon's shrine that they risked such dangers. The old world was divided into masters and servants. Gold offered them the chance to change that—to be free and independent and their own masters. To them Australia was not just the Land of Gold. It was the Land of Dreams.

> *Hurrah for Australia the Golden*
> *Where men of all nations now toil*
> *To none will we e'er be beholden*
> *While we've strength to turn up the soil*
> *There's no poverty here to distress us*
> *'Tis the country of true liberty*
> *No proud lords can ever oppress us*
> *But here we're untrammelled and free.*

High hopes were expressed and not just by the thousands of diggers who rushed to Kiandra after gold was discovered by prospectors late in 1859. There was newspaper talk of the Snowy River diggings as a golden storehouse, a new Ballarat, the richest field ever opened in New South

The Old Store and Post Office, Kiandra

Wales, which would not be exhausted for a century.

The Kiandra field was halfway between Sydney and Melbourne and the Governor of New South Wales, Sir William Denison, was anxious for Kiandra to restore the fortunes of New South Wales, which had become Victoria's poor sister in the days of gold. He wrote:

> The Kiandra diggings are to re-establish credit, make money plentiful, relieve the insolvents and find work for the unemployed.

For a short time those hopes seemed justified. By February in 1860 there were some twelve thousand diggers in the Kiandra area and in that year it produced sixty-eight thousand ounces of gold, the highest yield in New South Wales. But the first winter made clear what the diggers were up against and most of them left the field, although a thousand battled through that winter under canvas. The *Sydney Morning Herald* reported:

> It's a great warning in a region like Kiandra when you see skeletons of bullocks hanging in the trees up the side of high hills. The depth of the snow must be fearful when it is plainly shown by this that the cattle were feeding on the top branches of the trees.

Kiandra Goldfields

In this practically inaccessible country where there were no roads and supplies had to be laboriously brought in by packhorse, the diggers showed their typical spirit of improvisation. The Chinese found themselves in the unusual position of being a valued element on this field. They formed the Celestial Transport Company, a human pack-horse team which carried supplies up the last twenty kilometres to Kiandra and kept the town alive.

Australia's modern winter sports industry was born out of the Kiandra gold rush. The diggers found an answer to the snowy conditions with a device new to Australia—the ski. A Scandinavian miner named Bumpstone skied down the main street of Kiandra in 1861 and the idea quickly caught on. It wasn't quite skiing as we know it. Sometimes the miners sat astride a central pole which they used as a brake. The *Sydney Morning Herald* was agog:

> Down hill they can go as fast as a steamer and on the level, with the aid of the pole, they can make good headway.

The people found it was fun and they started organising snow carnivals, ski races, toboggan rides and they kept doing it long after the gold dwindled. They formed Australia's first ski club in 1878.

155

Skiers at Kiandra

Gold mining in various forms, like reefing, sluicing and dredging, struggled on at Kiandra till the turn of the century, but most of the surface alluvial gold had been exhausted within a year and when it disappeared, most of the diggers disappeared too. The heyday of the Kiandra goldfield was hectic and brief. It was notorious as a lawless and godless place with lots of violence and stickups and wild grog shanties run by dubious ladies like Brandy Mary and Roaring Mag.

Kiandra does not have much left to show from those wild days, but it established one tradition—the diggers would go anywhere and would endure any conditions as long as there was a good promise of gold. And it was this determination which expanded the frontiers of Australian settlement.

In 1867 sixteen thousand people rushed northwards to a remote gully of stinging Gympie-Gympie trees on the headwaters of the Mary River. The cause was gold and the discoverer was James Nash, a former Kiandra digger who had forsaken the snow to prospect the burning bush of Queensland.

Kiandra Mail

Gympie's gold monument commemorates James Nash and you could certainly say he deserved it. Queensland in 1867 was in a bad way. The economy was paralysed, the Treasury was broke and the unemployed were getting very restless. A desperate Government offered £3000 reward for the first discovery of payable gold and Nash obliged by producing seventy-five ounces from the nearby gully. The Government was so broke it could not even pay him the reward straight off. But their embarrassment soon vanished and Queensland's fortunes soon revived through the discovery of this rich field. It was briefly called Nashville, but it was soon known far and wide as Gympie.

The Queensland bush was a far cry from snowbound Kiandra, but conditions were just as harsh when the first diggers set up their tents on the Gympie field. Food was scarce, many diggers were quickly reduced to starvation and the alluvial gold gave out in a couple of years.

But unlike Kiandra, Gympie had rich quartz reefs. Queensland's first important goldfield went on producing gold until well into the twentieth century. It became an important provincial city, the home of many famous mines and one of the Big Three of Queensland's gold producers, along with Charters Towers and Mount Morgan.

The tide of settlement flowed northward with the gold rushes until it came to country which challenged the skills

of the hardest and toughest bushmen. The explorer Edmund Kennedy had been killed at Cape York by Aboriginals in 1848, and for a quarter of a century after, few white men had ventured into this hostile country. It was a bold prospector with the bold name of James Venture Mulligan who announced in September 1873 that his party had found payable gold, 102 ounces, on the Palmer River.

The rush that followed alarmed even Mulligan and he wrote to the *Queenslander* newspaper:

> I do wish to stop this before it grows any more. If people rush the place without rations, they must perish, for there is no getting back in the wet season across the rivers which lie between.

But Australian diggers had already shown they would brave hell and high water for gold. They were to get hell and high water on the Palmer. Within a month, hundreds rushed north from Mulligan's base at Georgetown. Within two months, thousands were arriving at a new port established by the Queensland government—Cooktown.

Above: *The Palmer River*
Top right: *Sovereign Hotel, Cooktown*
Bottom right: *Mount Morgan*

The wind is fair and free, my boys
The wind is fair and free
The steamer's course is north, my boys
And the Palmer we shall see
And the Palmer we shall see, my boys
And Cooktown's muddy shore
Where I've been told there's lots of gold
So stay down south no more.

So blow, ye winds, heigh-ho
A digging we will go
I'll stay no more down south, my boys
So let the music play
In spite of what I'm told
I'm off in search of gold
I'll make a push for that new rush
A thousand miles away.

Captain Cook beached his ship for repairs on the Endeavour River after he'd run onto a reef in 1770. There were no buildings there and there were still no buildings 103 years later when the news was announced of gold on the Palmer River. A short time after that announcement, ships were racing into the port from all over Australia, from New Zealand and from as far away as China. Cooktown became the highest and lustiest settlement on the eastern Australian coast, and spoke of itself freely as the Capital of Cape York.

Cooktown remains the highest settlement of any importance on the east coast and it still retains a certain air of rapscallion devil-may-care but it is only a shadow of that roaring gold port of a century ago. Thirty thousand people roistered through Charlotte Street with its hundreds of shops, its ninety-four pubs and its thriving bawdy houses run by French Charlie and Palmer Kate. And it all happened within a year of the arrival of the first ship from Brisbane, the *Leichhardt* which was hastily despatched by the Queensland Government with a party of gold officials, road engineers, police and hard-bitten diggers.

Spending the gold in Cooktown was no problem. Getting the gold from the Palmer was a problem. Getting *to* the Palmer was a problem that defied the road engineers who arrived with the first party of diggers and continues to defy road engineers to this day. Between Cooktown and the Palmer are 180 kilometres of some of the roughest country in the world. It is literally hell and high water—hellish hot

*Palmer diggers preparing
for defence*

in the tropical dry and impassable in the tropical wet. And
there were other hazards, as the first digger party that
struck out from Cooktown soon discovered.

The Palmer River in 1873 was Aboriginal land, far beyond the frontiers of white pastoral settlement. In this
country the black tribesmen hunted their game and caught
their fish and cherished their sacred places for thousands
of years. The invasion of gold diggers, swarming the
country and tearing up the rivers and creeks, burst on the
blacks like an atomic bomb. They did not comprehend
what the white men were grubbing for, but they saw their
own choice as either resistance or starvation, and they
chose to resist.

As a hundred-strong party led by Gold Warden St
George and road engineer MacMillan blazed their track
towards the Palmer, they camped one night at a place
known afterwards as Battle Camp. This is what happened,
in the words of one of the diggers, William Webb:

> About five next morning, 5th November, while the
> stars were still shining, a crowd of natives came up
> yelling a terrible war cry, and they reached to about
> 70 yards from where we lay all over the ground. There
> were about 40 in the first rank and as many more in
> reserve some distance behind. Just as the day was

161

breaking, MacMillan and St George advanced towards them. I noticed that they fired over the heads of the blacks, but some of the men fired straight at the blacks, some of whom fell. Thereupon the blacks ran away and were pursued as far as a large lagoon, and all that went there stayed there.

The blacks were cut to pieces by murderous fire from Snider rifles and they never again attacked the diggers head on. But Battle Camp was the start of a guerrilla war that was to go on for years, as the Palmer trails were blazed in blood.

The first track from Cooktown to the Palmer, opened by

A skirmish with the blacks

MacMillan's party, led by a roundabout route to Palmerville. But the gold rush quickly moved up river to a new centre, Maytown, and reports of rich alluvial pickings led to demands for a more direct track to Cooktown. A way was opened through Hell's Gates, which soon got a reputation which was as fiendish as its name. In the words of the *Queenslander:*

> If many of these rocks and defiles were endowed with speech, they could doubtless a tale unfold which would render the sound of Hell's Gates as horrifying to the ear as that of the dread region from which it is so justly named. At some future date the bush traveller or prospector may stumble on an abandoned camp of the Hell's Gates demons, and as he surveys with horror the ghostly relics lying around, his thoughts may revert to the old Palmer rush, and he will think with a shudder of those who perished miserably in the fierce race for wealth.

163

They were strong words. Hell's Gates is the sort of place that calls for strong words. Even today it is forbidding and desolate. In the 1870s it was an ideal place for an ambush and there were plenty. The most legendary black atrocity concerns the fate of the Macquarie brothers. The blacks captured them, killed the elder brother and roasted him to eat. The younger brother had to watch all this, because they cut his legs off and left him alive till they were ready. But before they came to kill him and eat him, he scratched the whole story with a piece of rock on a tin pannikin, and it was found by diggers a few days later. Or so the legend has it. The records of the inquest tell a different story.

The inquest was held at Cooktown Courthouse in February 1877. There were two key witnesses. One was John Rogan, who operated packhorses between Cooktown and the Palmer, like the Macquarie brothers, and had been following a few hours behind their packhorse team. Rogan described what he'd found at Hell's Gate—the remains of half-eaten packhorses and books and documents scattered on the ground.

Senior Constable Pickering, who had hurried from Cooktown to Hell's Gates, produced a number of grisly items he had found at the scene of the crime, including part of a blood-stained flannel shirt, a revolver, a hat, gold scales, letters, receipts and a carrier's licence made out to Hugh Macquarie, a canvas pack bag and gold bag—both empty—and the ashes of a fire:

> I found the pieces of hair produced in the ashes, one appeared to be from the head of a man and from the whiskers. I have shown it to Dr. Kortum and he pronounces it to be human hair. I also found two pieces of bone, and a substance which I believe to be burnt skin, which I now produce. I found no money during the five days search.

The magistrate, Alpin Cameron, made no comment and no finding. Perhaps he was pondering that last piece of evidence. The Macquaries had sold goods on the Palmer and must have been carrying money and gold. But no money was found and their gold bag was empty. These were not typical signs of a black attack.

The verdict of the newspapers was that the Macquaries had been slaughtered at Hell's Gates by a merciless mob of infuriated cannibals. It is true that the blacks killed about fifty white diggers on the Palmer and black cannibals were certainly not unknown there. But in the case of the Macquarie brothers, there was no explanation of the missing gold, which suggested a European crime. There was no evidence of a tin pannikin with all the horrible details scratched on it and this seems to have been a later invention—part of a propaganda war to justify the extermination of blacks who stood in the way of gold diggers. The slaughtering was mostly done by the white man's side.

Newspaper illustrations of the day seldom depicted the blacks at all, but they invariably depicted the whites as explorers and pioneers, battling their way through hostile bush for the greater glory of Australia. For a time the Palmer justified hopes that it would prove to be Queensland's richest goldfield, but the Palmer rush was not Australia's finest hour in race relations. The only common ground between the blacks and the whites was their hostility to a third race—the Chinese.

News of the Palmer River rush had reached China and the Chinese shipped direct to Cooktown in large numbers and walked to the Palmer where they met signs like this:

Any Chinaman found higher up this creek wil be instantly seized and hanged until he is dead.

By 1877 there were nearly eighteen thousand Chinese on the Palmer against less than two thousand white diggers and their industry and sheer numbers kept up the gold production figures for a couple of years. But there was a savage backlash from the outnumbered whites and the Queensland Government passed laws imposing an entry tax on Chinese, preventing them from going to new goldfields and increasing their miner's right from ten shillings to three pounds a year. The increase had to be withdrawn when the Chinese couldn't pay it. By the end of the 1870s they were not making that kind of money and neither was anyone else on the Palmer. The alluvial riches had been cleaned out.

One of the Chinese diggers was Tam Sze Poy, who later left the goldfields to open his store in Innisfail. His diary, kept by his grandson, reveals that the Palmer was no picnic for Chinese:

There was a rumour then that gold had been discovered in a place called Cooktown, the source of which was inexhaustible and free to all. Oh! what disappointment when we learnt that the rumour was unfounded and we were misled. Not only was the gold

165

Ida Mine, Maytown

difficult to find, but the climate was not suitable and was the cause of frequent attacks and illness. As we went about there met our gaze the impoverished condition and the starved looks of our fellow countrymen. I now realise that to search for gold was like trying to catch the moon at the bottom of the sea. Forsaking it for something else, I worked in a restaurant at the wages of 2 pounds a month. It was six years since we first came but we had accomplished nothing.

Maytown was the capital of the Palmer goldfield. Today it presents the picture of a gold rush town which has gone back to the bush, leaving legends of easy fortunes for a few and hardship and death for many. Rusty machinery tells of the battle to establish reef mining on the Palmer with mines like the Ida, Louisa, King of the Ranges and Queen of the North. The battle was lost, not for lack of reef gold, but for lack of capital and machinery and transportation and skilled manpower, on an impossibly remote field where freight costs were prohibitive and disease and the wet ambushed more diggers than the blacks ever did.

An overgrown track is all there is to show of the main street, Leslie Street. Once it boasted twelve hotels, where

Railway Bridge, Laura

it was said more money was spent over the bars than in any town in the North. There is nothing now to suggest that a million ounces of gold were won there in just five years.

The most powerful symbol of the hopes and eventual disillusionment of the Palmer is the railway bridge at Laura—part of a line from Cooktown that was to open up Cape York. Unfortunately it was built ten years too late and the engine that steamed across the bridge to test it in 1888 was the first and last train ever to cross the bridge. The Palmer was finished, the line was abandoned, the bridge was swept away by floods and the forlorn arches at Laura are monuments to a forgotten dream.

There are still no proper roads into the Palmer and it remains harsh and primitive country. But the great rush of people to the Palmer vastly accelerated the settlement of North Queensland, the expansion of the pastoral, sugar and tin mining industries and the foundation of important cities like Cairns. And the Australian digger had established yet again that he would tramp through the gates of hell for gold.

By the 1880s goldrushes had drawn Australian diggers as far north as Cape York, as far south as Tasmania. From South Australia they had trekked through the centre of the continent to the Northern Territory in the wake of the Overland Telegraph Line. In 1885 they were drawn across the top of Australia, from the Pacific to the Indian Ocean, by Western Australia's first payable gold strike at Hall's Creek in the Kimberleys. It was dry country. A publican there said:

You remember that spell of rain when it fell down for forty days and forty nights, and Noah built that ark?

Well, here at Hall's Creek we got fifteen points.

Within a couple of years new gold finds pulled the gold trail southwards from the Kimberleys through the Pilbara field and Marble Bar to the Murchison and its capital, Cue. The town was named after its first prospector, Tom Cue, and a rotunda marks the site where the diggers struck something as precious as gold in that country—water at twenty-five metres down. It bears the inscription:

In honour of the pioneers of the Murchison. With water bag and pick they converted an inhospitable desert and carved out happy and prosperous towns.

Cue was one of those happy and prosperous towns. It produced one and a half million ounces of gold from mines like the Hidden Treasure, the Golden Stream, the Light of Asia and the Gem of Cue. At one stage it had 7000 people and eleven hotels. It styled itself the Queen of the Murchison and it was quite a stylish place, where ladies wore gowns and gloves and carried parasols.

But the diggers didn't really convert an inhospitable desert. They battled with it as long as there was gold to be had and they invented their own methods of crossing the trackless and waterless wastes. They pushed wheelbarrows big enough to carry their mining equipment, tents, provisions and water. It took enormous strength to push the cumbersome machines sometimes for hundreds of miles, but many of the diggers had enormous strength.

The most legendary of the western barrowmen was Russian Jack, a giant of a man over two metres tall who built and operated an equally great barrow with shafts over two metres long. Russian Jack wheeled his barrow from Derby to the Kimberley rush and later to the Murchison rush at Cue and there are many stories of him coming across exhausted diggers in the desert and piling them on his barrow and wheeling them to the nearest well.

Russian Jack was a good-hearted giant, but given to the grog. It is said that he was once leaving Cue drunk with his barrow full of dynamite. The police arrested him for his own safety and chained him to a big log while they went off on other business. When they came back Russian Jack was gone. They found him in the nearest bar, leaning against the log which he had picked up and carried inside. He was quiet enough but they say that when he whispered his order to the barmaid, the glasses rattled on the shelf behind her.

The Australian gold rushes of the nineteenth century had drawn new trails across the country and planted new centres of population in just forty years. The pattern was completed in the land of gold in 1892 when diggers dashed down from the Murchison field and across from the eastern states to a dazzling new goldfield—Coolgardie.

Arthur Bayley was a typical model of the roving Australian digger. He'd chased gold on the Palmer River and the Murchison. With a mate, William Ford, he set out to prospect in little known country 500 kilometres east of Perth:

> We reached Coolgardie at 5 p.m. and in the morning we went out for the horses in order to give them a drink. I was leading my horse over what was later called Fly Flat when I picked up a piece of gold, weighing half an ounce. I think we were more excited about that bit of gold than any we found afterwards.

The excitement was just beginning. Bayley and Ford quickly discovered a rich shaft of gold at Coolgardie. They rode to the nearest settlement, Southern Cross, to file their reward claim and when they came back to Coolgardie they were followed by hundreds and within weeks by thousands of diggers. It was the start of the biggest and richest gold rush in the West.

Fly Flat quickly became an ant-heap of shafts and tents as diggers beavered away for the plentiful alluvial gold. Once again they found the major battle was not for wealth but for survival. Gold was plentiful but water was scarce in one of the most arid regions of Australia. Dust, disease and death were the grim companions of the first Coolgardie miners and many of them found early graves in the Golden West. A correspondent to the *Bulletin* reported:

A land of wearisome monotony, of crooked scrub, of sad-coloured bushes, of low flatcrested ridges—a grassless, waterless waste. Even in paradoxical Australia, it seems like a cynical criticism of Fate that this unpromising area should have been selected as the scene of the latest gold craze. Good men, tried pioneers who have known hardship in the fever-haunted gullies of the Palmer and the diamond fields of South Africa, are there. For one lucky man there are more than a hundred unfortunates, and somewhere about 4000 people are now wondering why on earth they ever came to such a God-forsaken country.

The diggers didn't have enough water to wash themselves in and, more important from their point of view, they didn't have enough water to wash gold in. With their typical spirit of improvisation they found a way around that, and invented the dry blower, a machine that trapped the gold while it shook and blew away the dust. But finding water fit to drink was another matter. Conditions were so

Miner's camp in the bush, Kalgoorlie

bad in the early months of Coolgardie that people were advised to leave the field for their own survival. Those who stayed on had to rely for food and water on teamsters who cursed the Coolgardie track:

> *Damn Coolgardie! Damn the track!*
> *Damn the goldfields, there and back!*
> *Damn the flies and damn the weather*
> *Damn the country altogether!*

Primitive goldfields hospitals sprang up and their beds were quickly filled. There were nearly 200 deaths from typhoid in the first two years of Coolgardie and sickness was rife from bad water, bad hygiene and a diet consisting almost entirely of tinned meat or, as the diggers cynically called it, tinned dog.

Whatever Coolgardie is going to be in the coming winter, it is represented just now by a wretched handful of galvanised iron calico and bag shanties, set down in the middle of a drought-bound, God-abandoned, sore-eyed, howling wilderness of dust, thirst and desolation, where water is a shilling a gallon and nothing obtainable in the shape of food except tinned

172

meat (the mainstay of W.A.) and preserves, at the usual goldfields prices.

A solution of sorts to the water problem was found by building condensers to convert salt water from the salt-pans to fresh water. But the results were pretty disgusting and the water cost the diggers more than they had to pay for whisky or gin. Away from the condensers, in the desert country, a man's only friend was his waterbag and diggers who rushed to remote gold strikes had to risk the consequences.

In the case of one rush to a place aptly named Siberia, fifty miners had to rely for water on one small soak which quickly dried up. Mr Renou, the Water Supply Official at Coolgardie, heard about their plight and sent out teams with water supplies, but for some it was too late. The bodies of ten diggers were found, perished in the bush.

Despite the incredible hardships of its beginnings, Coolgardie became a very considerable city. Within six years of the first gold find by Bayley and Ford, Coolgardie had 15 000 people, three breweries, seven newspapers and two stock exchanges. An International Mining and Mineral Exhibition in 1899 attracted 60 000 people.

The scale of Coolgardie's remaining buildings gives some idea of the scale of their thinking and their optimism in the 1890s. The main street, Bayley Street, was a magnificent thoroughfare, broad enough to allow a camel team to turn around in, in a forward sweep, because the camels wouldn't go in reverse. That was just one of the camel's peculiar characteristics. They were spoken of with contempt:

> The camel in Western Australia is an ill-conditioned, mangey horror with a temper as short as his coat. At any period of the day, if he can safely bite a piece out of you or kick you in the stomach, he does so at once. At dawn he commences to whine and curse profanely in his own language, and continues his blasphemy all through the process of loading. Put a postage stamp on his back over and above the load he usually carries and he would sooner die and give you the trouble of disposing of his corpse than get up. It is only when you become acquainted with a camel that you appreciate the lovable qualities of horse, bullock or dog.

And yet these contrary and unlovable creatures were the saviours of many a digger in the early days of Coolgardie.

173

With their hardy Afghan drivers, some 2000 camels crossed the waterless wastes with vital supplies of food, water and equipment. And sometimes they were enlisted as a means of family transport. Lone diggers and those who could not afford horses or camels, continued to rely on their homemade wheelbarrows, which they were ever ready to trundle across the desert at the slightest hint of a new rush.

But perhaps the most characteristic vehicles on the Western goldfields were bicycles. They required neither water nor grass and many diggers used them to get around in the flat country. The key users were the special despatch riders who sped across the goldfields delivering urgent mail and mining notices and hot gossip. Their fast and reliable services were extensively advertised in the papers and the Coolgardie Cycle Express Company even put out its own stamps till this practice was vetoed by the Post Office.

Londonderry Mine

The specials had plenty of work in the 1890s as continuing news of West Australian gold strikes excited London investors and millions of pounds of British capital poured into the field to develop reef mining. It was a heyday for company promotions. For two years new West Australian gold mining companies were born in London at the rate of one a day. In just one month, April 1896, eighty-one new gold mining companies were floated on the London stock exchange.

Unfortunately a lot of them were fiascos or frauds. The most notorious case was the Londonderry Mine. A party of six eastern States prospectors discovered this apparently rich shaft near Coolgardie in 1894. In a month's work they took 8000 ounces of gold out of the mine. They had only dug a hole the size of a grave when they accepted an offer of £180 000 for the mine from Lord Fingall on behalf of an English syndicate.

There was a handover ceremony at the mine. Most of Coolgardie's leading citizens were present. Lord Fingall and others made flowery speeches about the fabulous prospects of this hole of gold and some declared it would be the richest mine in the universe. Twelve bags of quartz obviously bulging with gold were taken out for display in London before the hole was sealed up and fenced off, with a guard stationed to ensure that nobody got at it.

The samples made such an impression in London that the unprecedented sum of £700 000 in shares was subscribed in a matter of days. Only £50 000 of this was earmarked to develop the mine, but the company directors explained that it would not need any more. If the gold continued at the same rate as the first few feet of the shaft it would pay £15 000 000.

But when Lord Fingall returned to open up the mine, he made a most unpleasant discovery and on April Fool's Day, 1895, he was forced to cable London:

> Regret in extreme have to inform you that rich shoots of ore opened very bad indeed; does not appear to be practically anything important left.

Under the heading 'The Londonderry Fiasco' the *Economist* expressed the outrage of the London investors:

> There has been no instance of such a complete falsification of early promises as that of the Londonderry in the recent history of mining, and it can scarcely be wondered at that some of the shareholders entertain the suspicion that the property had been salted before it was visited by Lord Fingall ... The Londonderry Mine was spoken of as a sort of bullion vault, from which the gold could be literally shovelled out ... Why should the original owners of the property have been anxious to dispose of it, if there was this untold wealth within their grasp? We can only trust that the lessons of the Londonderry incident will not readily be forgotten.

It was never satisfactorily established whether the Londonderry was an honest mistake or a hoax, a Golden Fleece, but it was not the only dubious proposition on the Western goldfields. A correspondent to the *Bulletin* sounded this warning note:

> For miles around Coolgardie proper and the outlying fields, the country is held under mining leases, ninetenths of which are as free from gold as a frog from feathers. Others again have yielded a few hundred ounces to the lucky finders (by hand crushing) and now show a fair prospect, evidently left for the inspec-

tion of intending speculators.

The local paper, the *Coolgardie Miner* put the case more bluntly:

> A Coolgardie Mining Liar is one of the most stupendous works of nature. He scatters forged data and fabricated facts around in a loose and lordly style, that paralyses a new arrival and makes ordinary perverters of the truth, such as lawyers and politicians, feel their insignificance in the very first act.

Too many Londonderries and confidence and the flow of British capital might have quickly failed. But it never did chiefly because of a discovery by three Irish prospectors on a hill forty kilometres east of Coolgardie.

The Irishmen, Hannan, Flanagan and Shea were on their way from Coolgardie to a so-called prospect at Mount Youlle when one of their horses threw a shoe and they had to make camp on the slopes of Mount Charlotte. Paddy Hannan, like every good prospector, kept his eyes down, picked up lumps of gold and started the richest gold rush in Australian history. The place was first called Hannan's Rush, but it was soon known the world over by its native name—Kalgoorlie.

The real treasures of Kalgoorlie were not on the slopes where Paddy Hannan picked up his gold but far under them in rich lodes which went down and down into the earth. This was the famous Golden Mile, the richest square mile of gold on planet Earth. For Australia Kalgoorlie was a golden milestone, the greatest find since Ballarat and Bendigo. And like Ballarat and Bendigo it changed the course of Australian history.

Before gold the huge State of Western Australia, one-third of the continent, had less than 40 000 people—less than the population of Ballarat. Gold quadrupled the population of the West in ten years and most of the new population were Australians from the eastern States—T'Other Siders, as they were called in Kalgoorlie.

They believed in a single Australian nation and they forced a reluctant West Australian government to join the Australian Federation by threatening to form an independent state, Auralia, unless a Federation referendum was held in the west. In that referendum it was the goldfields vote which won the day for Federation, under the slogan 'One People, One Flag, One Destiny'.

It was the economic and population strength of the gold-

Left: *Mount Charlotte, Kalgoorlie*
Opposite top: *Exchange Hotel, Kalgoorlie*
Opposite bottom: *The Golden Mile*

fields which forced the West Australian government to solve the water problem once and for all by building the water pipeline from Mundaring Weir to Kalgoorlie in one of the great feats of Australian engineering. And it was the continuing productivity of the western goldfields which made possible the Transcontinental Railway linking Australia for the first time by rail from coast to coast.

The statue of Paddy Hannan with his waterbag gazes on modern Kalgoorlie wistfully. It became a big company, deep-mining field, no place for small-time diggers. Paddy

himself saw little of the gold and died a pensioner. But he left a monument more imposing than his statue.

Hannan Street is the impressive main street of a city founded on the fortunes of gold. And the gold won from Kalgoorlie helped sustain Australia's fortunes through major depressions in the 1890s and the 1930s. Many families on the breadline in eastern Australia survived those dark days because of the money orders sent by husbands, brothers and sons from the Kalgoorlie Post Office.

The story of Australian gold production in the twentieth century is very largely the story of Kalgoorlie's Golden Mile. Western Australia has produced three-quarters of Australian gold in this century and much of it has come from the Golden Mile, the richest single goldfield in our history. The shafts and the head frames and the great slime dumps are the trademarks of an industry which gave Australians jobs in hard times when everything else looked hopeless.

The Golden Mile itself has had its hard times. Australia is no longer a major producer of gold and gold no longer dominates our economy as it once did. Which is perhaps just as well with the world price of gold going up and down like a yo-yo in recent years. The Golden Mile battles on, but the major battle these days is to calculate the cost of recovering the gold from the Kalgoorlie deeps against the chance of selling it for a profit.

The new face of Australian gold mining in the 1980s is the Telfer Mine, operated by Newmont and BHP and currently the biggest gold producer in Australia. Telfer is far out in the Great Sandy Desert of Western Australia, in the Pilbara country where the old prospectors wheeled their barrows. But they wouldn't find much to recognise at the Telfer Mine. Neither would the traditional deep miners of Bendigo and Kalgoorlie.

Telfer is an open-cut mine, a great open crater where the ore is scooped up by front-end loaders. The key to the success of the operation is total mechanisation and massive throughput of ore. In 1981 the mine produced 130 857 ounces of gold for revenue of thirty million dollars and net profit of $10.8 million.

Gold has always had a way of turning up in the most remote and inhospitable places and they don't come much more remote than Telfer. The nearest town of any size,

Port Hedland, is nearly 500 kilometres away. But Telfer is no wildcat show operated by prospectors on a shoestring. It is a company town and the company has imported its own civilisation to the spot. There is a village to accommodate 300 people in air-conditioned houses with landscaped gardens and there are community facilities like a supermarket, a primary school and social facilities to ease the pain of isolation in the desert.

Not everybody can take this kind of life and the work force is only selected after careful screening. There are compensations—the money is good and the trucks have automatic gears, hydraulic assistance, air-conditioning and sound proofing. Everything is up to date at Telfer City. There's an on-site computer to assess ore values and reserves, and a complete treatment plant to process the ore, separate the gold and pour it in 400-ounce bars which are flown down to the Perth Mint.

The Perth Mint was built in the 1890s at the time of the great discoveries in the Golden West. Nowadays Kalgoorlie's gold, Telfer's gold and ninety per cent of all Australian gold is sold to the Perth Mint for refining. It says something about the allure and fascination of gold that some of the Mint's gold refining methods are as old as civilisation and were practised by the ancient Egyptians, while others are as new as the Space Age.

All incoming parcels of gold are weighed on the balance and assayed to measure their content of pure gold. With computer equipment this can be estimated in a matter of seconds and the seller is paid according to the going rate for gold that day. Then the mint sets about its job of refining the gold, by heating it to over 1000 degrees centigrade in crucibles and bubbling chlorine gas through it. All other metals attach themselves to the bubbles and float to the surface as chlorides. They are scraped off the surface after several hours, and samples of the molten gold are examined under X-ray fluorescent spectroscopes to see if they have reached the accepted world standard of purity for gold, which is 99.5 per cent. When this standard is reached the gold is poured into moulds and set into 400-ounce bars. The bars are then cleaned with acid, stamped with the Mint's special symbol and assay number and stored as fine gold or bullion.

Some of this gold is used for special purposes, like the

Right: *The Perth Mint*
Opposite top: *Blasting at Telfer*
Opposite bottom: *Telfer*

production of commemorative medals. The rest is sold to jewellers, dentists, industry and the Gold Producers' Association.

The Mint buys most of its gold from big mining companies, but it still receives regular parcels from small miners. The day of the little digger and the lone prospector has not ended in Australia and it will never end as long as finds like the Hand of Faith nugget are made. Weighing twenty-seven kilograms, or 720 troy ounces, it is the biggest nugget found in Australia in recent times. It was found in September 1980 and proudly exhibited on television by the

Victorian Premier, Mr Hamer. But unfortunately no buyer was found in Australia and it was sold to a Las Vegas saloon for a million dollars. The Hand of Faith was found in Victoria's Golden Triangle at Kingower near Wedderburn. A spare-time prospector named Kevin Hillier found the nugget with the aid of a metal detector, and metal detectors have since uncovered other valuable nuggets in the same area.

An old-time prospector once said sarcastically:
   The beauty of prospecting as a profession is that so
   little is needed to pursue it. Beyond a knowledge of
   mineralogy, metallurgy, physics, map reading, navi-
   gation and bushcraft, one need know absolutely
   nothing.
Metal detectors have certainly made the prospector's job
a bit easier. All over Australia the search for gold is con-

tinued by individuals and small syndicates. Some use new-fangled methods like bulldozing layers of earth and then scanning the soil with metal detectors. Some sluice and dredge the rivers and streams. Some rely on the fashioned methods of shaft and windlass. And some operate their own crushers in the remote mountains where gold has been found for a hundred years. The urge to find gold is as strong as ever.

The urge, or fever, began at Ophir when Hargraves panned his first specks of gold and Lister and Tom found the first payable gold in 1851. Those discoveries totally changed the face and the image of Australia. The land of sheep and squires and convicts suddenly became the Land of Gold and the shining Eldorado of the common man.

Gold destroyed the old social fabric of masters and servants. It brought new people and new ideas. The continuous gold rushes stretched Australian settlement to every corner of the continent. In the century after Ophir Australia produced 170 million ounces of gold, worth at today's values sixty-eight thousand million dollars and that massive wealth largely propelled Australia into modern nationhood.

Perhaps the most interesting effect of gold was on the Australian character. It wasn't always a pretty story. There was plenty of skullduggery and bloodshed and tragedy and that old greed for gold is still reflected in our materialistic society. But there was also a spirit of give it a go, no matter how unlikely the odds.

The story is told of the Australian gold digger who went to Heaven. St Peter said, 'I'm sorry mate, there's no room. The place is full of Australian diggers.' The old timer said, 'I'll fix that,' and he shouted, 'Gold! There's been a gold strike in Hell!' In a moment the gates burst open and Heaven was emptied. Next thing St Peter noticed the old digger was rolling his swag and getting ready to leave, and he said, 'What are you doing? You know you started that rumour.' The old digger said, 'I know I did, Pete, but it just occurred to me there might be something in it.'

You can call it unquenchable optimism, a mystic belief in the Lucky Strike and the pot of gold at the end of the rainbow. Or you can call it a humorous gamble with the lottery of fate. I think it is still in the Australian character and it came to us from gold.

Index